A Young Person's Guide
to Classical Music

A Young Person's Guide to Classical Music
by
Earl Ofari Hutchinson

PRESS

A Young Person's Guide to Classical Music

Copyright © 2022 Earl Ofari Hutchinson
All rights reserved including the right of reproduction in whole or in part in any form.

Printed in the United States

Published by
Middle Passage Press
5517 Secrest Drive
Los Angeles, California 90043

Copyediting and Graphic Design by Alan Bell
Index by Middle Passage Press Index Services

Publisher's Cataloging-in-Publication Data

Names: Hutchinson, Earl Ofari, author.
Title: A young person's guide to classical music / Earl Ofari Hutchinson.
Description: Los Angeles, CA : Middle Passage Press, 2022. | Includes bibliographic references and index. | Summary: Easy-to-understand primer on classical music, including history, musical terms, and how to listen to and appreciate the music.
Identifiers: LCCN X | ISBN 9781881032205 (pbk.)
Subjects: LCSH: Music appreciation—Juvenile literature. | Music—Analysis, interpretation, appreciation—Juvenile literature. | Music—History and criticism—Juvenile literature. | BISAC: MUSIC / Genres & Styles / Classical. | MUSIC / History & Criticism. | MUSIC / Instruction & Study / Appreciation.
Classification: LCC MT6.H88 2022| DDC 781.68 H—dc23
LC record available at https://lccn.loc.gov/X

Library of Congress Control Number:
Middle Passage Press, Los Angeles, California

Table of Contents

1	Introduction
10	The Classical Music Periods
32	The Symphony
49	The Concerto
63	The Opera
82	The Smaller Works
96	The Instruments
109	The Soloist
118	Conclusion
127	Notes
138	Index
147	Bibliography
150	Talking the Classical Music's Jargon
154	About the Author

Dedication
Thank You
Lenny
Leonard Bernstein

A Young Person's Guide
to Classical Music

Introduction

"Why are young people not listening to classical music?"
What's turning young people off classical music concerts?
Why teens don't listen to classical music
Why do young people express a dislike for classical music?

These four questions are not really questions. They are the title of four lengthy music and arts articles in journals and publications from 2017 to 2021. They pose and then try to answer the question that's been fiercely and seemingly endlessly debated among classical music writers, scholars, musicians, and concert masters. The question has even greater urgency for concert orchestra board of directors, administrators, and officials. For them, it's a question of dollars. Put simply, the fewer people that fill concert halls means steadily dwindling revenue.

Classical musical audiences are getting older, and older. If they are not replaced by a new crop of younger listeners that means more empty seats, and even less revenue. At the same time, costs to run an orchestra, pay staff and management, and the musicians, aren't going down. Eventually, there's a break point. The result could be staff cutbacks, fewer concerts, and in some cases orchestras folding completely.

One especially gloomy classical music doomsayer went further. The headline of his piece said it all, "It's Time to Let Classical Music Die." His particular gripe was the seeming lack of ethnic diversity within classical music orchestras. He contended that this was a big reason why so many young and not so young persons are the disappearing act in classical music.

Loads of reasons have been given for the apparent absence of young persons from the concert halls. The concerts are too long, too boring, you must sit still interminably long in stone silence. You certainly can't dance and sing to a symphony. It's also said concerts are too costly, and too robotic. The more charitable answer is that young persons aren't regularly exposed to the music. Many public schools have cut back arts programs and instruction, eliminated field trips to concert halls, and invitations to classical musicians to perform at schools. There is some truth to all these explanations for the non-appearance of young people in the classical music concert halls.

Introduction

* * * * *

It wasn't always that way. There are two pictures that I still have a vivid memory of. One is a group of smiling, cheery looking teens and pre-teens huddled around English composer Benjamin Britten (1913-1976). The picture was on the cover of an album cut jointly with the English Chamber Orchestra and the London Symphony Orchestra. The album was released in 1946. The featured work was Britten's famed *The Young Person's Guide to the Orchestra*.

The work was first publicly performed in October 1946. The work was commissioned by the British Ministry of Education for a documentary film. This fit a pattern in classical music going back to its formal beginning in the 17th Century. From there through much of the 19th Century, the kings, queens, church royalty, and wealthy patrons of the arts commissioned classical works. The big guns in classical music—Mozart, Haydn, Bach, Beethoven, and Haydn made their living off commissions for their work. They spun that off into well paid performances for the gatherings of the nobility.

Britten's work had a three-fold aim. One was to showcase a very listenable and playable musical work. The second was to showcase the various instruments in a symphonic orchestra. The third and most important was to stir interest in young persons in classical music.

Even at that time there was mounting concern that the vast changes in the immediate post World War II period in England and globally would have an adverse impact on music and the arts. A new generation would have zero interest in a music that was typed by many as music from a dead past. Britten and the ministry's answer was to give them a basic work, make it enjoyable, and spotlight the instruments with the hope that this might stir the interest of some young persons.

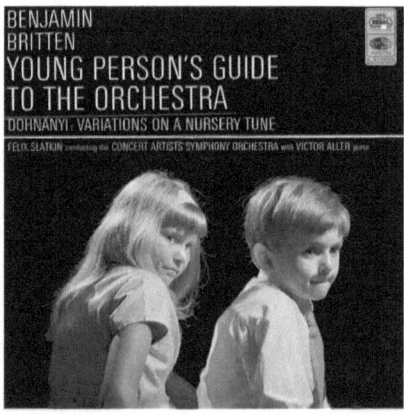

Recommended Listening

Benjamin Britten, *The Young Person's Guide to the Orchestra*, Op. 34
WDR Symphony Orchestra
www.youtube.com/watch?v=4vbvhU22uAM

* * * * *

The second picture I vividly remember is of a poster at the entrance to New York's Carnegie Hall. Pictured were several persons accompanied by their parents walking into the hall for a performance. The poster read "Young People's Concert." Underneath that was the name "Leonard Bernstein." The year was 1960. Bernstein was two years into his tenure as music director of the New York Philharmonic Orchestra.

In the next decade under his tutelage the orchestra would be widely acclaimed as America's flagship orchestra. Bernstein had the idea that to interest young persons in classical music he'd have to tailor concerts just for them. He'd conduct the orchestra, maybe play a piece on the piano, and then explain in laypersons terms what he played and what to listen for in the piece. Bernstein called this his "educational mission."

 **Recommended Listening**

Leonard Bernstein, Vol. 1, 17 Episodes
New York Philharmonic
www.youtube.com/watch?v=WmfbVThu_i0

Bernstein had a huge advantage. He had television. CBS liked the idea of Bernstein playing, talking about the music, and conducting the orchestra all the while schooling the kids and their parents on what an orchestra actually did and how to listen to the music. Even after Bernstein stepped down as music director in 1969, he kept coming back to his passion which was the series and talking to young people about classical music.

Courtesy of CBS an entire generation through the 1960s and into the early 1970s in person and on TV, watched with awe and fascination Bernstein take a complex aspect of classical music and make it simple and intelligible for a kid to understand. I was one of those young persons fascinated watching Bernstein talk about a music that I had absolutely no knowledge of, or then, barely knew existed. Here was guy who knew exactly how to make the music come alive and mean something to a youngster.

The program elevated classical music from something that many saw as a stodgy formalistic, music for the elite, or old people. produced by mostly long dead European men. Bernstein made the music a music that was understandable and popular.

The program ran for 14 years. During that time, he put on 53 concerts. He covered most of the musical bases, introduced many talented young virtuoso performers who went on to become mega-stars in the classical music world. He kept a generation of young persons educated and enthralled with classical music.

From the Concert Seat

One of my fun weekends was at the world-renowned Aspen Music Festival in Aspen, Colorado. It's an annual month-long event that features an almost round the clock program of symphonies, chamber works, master classes and lectures on every aspect of classical music. I mingled with and interviewed musicians and the administrative staff of the festival.

My biggest thrill was watching and listening to the training orchestras playing some of the greatest classical works. They brought so much energy, passion, and just plain fun to the music that it was infectious. The added plus for me was that the orchestras looked like a little United Nations. There were African Americans, Hispanics, Asians, and Mid-Eastern musicians. I knew from this that the future of classical music was in good hands.

* * * * *

This is a good time to make a crucial point. There is no miracle or magic formula to get masses of young persons rushing to classical music concerts. Classical music is no different than any other music, rock, pop, reggae, R&B, rap, jazz, country and western, bluegrass, and other musical genres from everywhere else on the planet. It has its rabid fans, rabid detractors, and a great majority in the middle ground who could care less about the music one way or the other. It's a matter of choice, taste, and to a degree exposure.

A Young Person's Guide to Classical Music is not an attempt to make new converts to classical music. It's certainly not an attempt to duplicate, let alone match the kind of passion expertise, and professionalism Bernstein and Britten spurred young persons to listen to and even love classical music back in their day. In any case, there's not an aspect of classical music that hasn't been written about, in more instances than not repeatedly. The books on classical music fill dozens of public and private library and bookstore shelves.

I make no pretense that this book is a comprehensive, touch all bases, work on classical music. My goal was a fast paced, highly readable basic primer for those young persons interested in classical music or want to develop an interest in it. It's a layperson's guide to common musical terms, instruments, selected composers, influential works, the styles, form and structure common to classical music. I present a capsulized history of the different periods in classical music's evolution.

I include a number of important compositions from different periods of the music's evolution as recommended listening. I toss in a few interesting factoids about the best-known composers and their works. I also squeeze in the sections "From the Concert Seat," some interesting and amusing tidbits about the composers, the instruments, and their works.

I end with some thoughts on what can spur interest in more young persons in classical music. Again, my aim is not to proselytize young people on the music, it's to try to make classical music and its components understandable—for those interested.

Years after his last Young People's Concert, Bernstein reflected on their importance. He called them "among my favorite, most highly prized activities of my life."

I'd like to think this book in a modest way accomplishes the same goal.

1

The Classical Music Periods

"I did think I did see all heaven before me and the great God himself."

George Frideric Handel (1685-1759) said that. It is one of the most cited quotes from any composer about their work. The work he thanked God and the heavens for is one of the best known of any classical works. It is also considered one of the gold standards of the period when classical music began to come into its own.

Handel gave divine thanks the moment he completed *Messiah* (1741). Handel, Johann Sebastian Bach (1685-1750), and Antonio Vivaldi (Italy, 1678-1741) are the A team headliners for the first defined period in classical music-the **Baroque** period. It ran roughly from 1600 to 1750. There's even a spin-off period within this period. It's called the **High Baroque**. That being true, what else could it be called but High. This is when the Baroque style of classical music hit its peak when Handel, Bach, and Vivaldi wrote their most significant works.

Now according to the *Merriam-Webster Dictionary*, there are three official definitions of the Baroque and the musical style it spawned. One is, "It's variously of, relating to, or having the characteristics of a style of artistic expression prevalent, especially in the 17th century that is marked generally by the use of complex forms, bold ornamentation, and the juxtaposition of contrasting elements often conveying a sense of drama, movement, and tension."

The second is, "It's characterized by grotesque, extravagance, complexity, or flamboyance. "This is my favorite of the three; the literal definition, "It's irregularly shaped—used of gems—a baroque pearl."

The Baroque period is the key to understanding what came after in classical music and remains today. The significant composers at the start of this new, innovative sound were two early Italian operatic and **madrigal** composers, Jacopo Peri (Italy, 1561-1633) and Claudio Monteverdi (Italy, 1567-1643). They used new instruments and musical forms such as **basso continuo** (continuous bass) and **recitative** (talk, talk, and more talk). This is one of the distinguishing features of the early Baroque period in opera.

Madrigal. This is a secular vocal number with no instruments for two to eight singers.

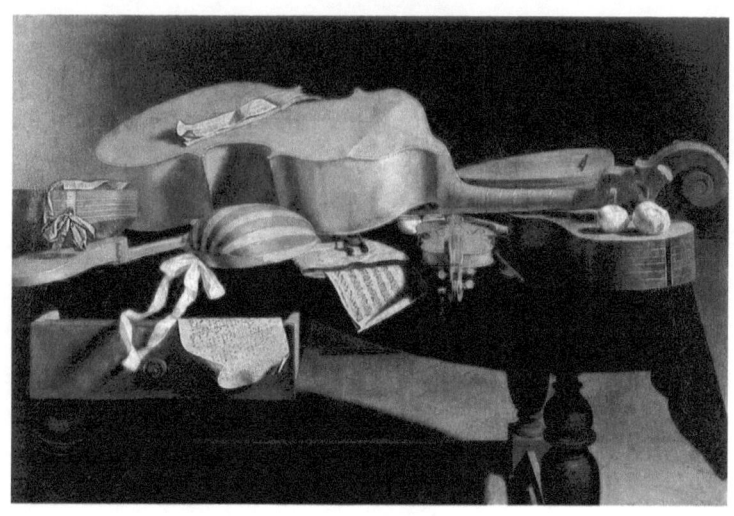

Recommended Listening

Johann Pachelbel, *Canon in D Major*
London Symphony Orchestra
www.youtube.com/watch?v=8Af372EQLck

Bach, Vivaldi, and Georg Telemann (1681-1767) did not write opera. They did write religious-themed works and purely instrumental works for small ensembles. However, they and the Baroque opera composers wrestled with the problem of how to make their works as compelling as possible to the audience. They focused on using the new style to draw out the range of human emotions—joy, sorrow, anger, love, fear, etc. (affections).

There was a lot of variety to choose from—concert

madrigals—one or more voices and occasionally with instruments, and the sacred concertos—a sacred vocal work with instruments. The composers now had a lot more freedom to make their music as free sounding as possible to increase opera's sound and dramatic action and thereby generate greater audience appeal.

Here's the closing line in the summary of the section in one of the college texts that is considered one of the Bibles of classical music, *A History of Western Music*, "For many listeners today Bach and Handel are the Baroque." Volumes, of course, have been written on Bach and Handel and their immense influence on Western music—not just classical—but pop, rock and roll, country, opera, and so forth. When asked about western music and composing, Johannes Brahms (1833-1897) simply said, "Study Bach. There you will find everything."

Ludwig von Beethoven (1770-1827) said of Handel, "He is the greatest composer that ever lived. I would uncover my head and kneel before his tomb." Wolfgang Amadeus Mozart (1833-1897) also said of Handel, "Handel understands effect better than any of us—when he chooses, he strikes like a thunderbolt."

The praise of Bach and Handel especially coming from Beethoven, Mozart, and Brahms, was not mere hero worship. It reflected their deep appreciation of, and the influence on their music, of the Baroque masters.

* * * * *

Despite the mountains of accolades showered on them through the centuries, neither Bach nor Handel created an original musical form. Handel's operas and oratorios and Bach's **cantatas, masses, oratorios, keyboard,** and **violin concertos** were cobbled together from Italian, French, German, and other musical forms. They include the old works—madrigals, Italian and French operas, orchestral suites, and keyboard music. But then again, what they borrowed or pilfered from these sources, they did it a lot different, a whole lot better, and with a whole lot more sophisticated styling.

Cantata features soloists, a choir or chorus, and an orchestra and is often a religious-themed work.
Mass is a choral sacred musical composition.
Oratorio is a tremendous musical work for orchestra and voices with a religious theme. Think Handel's *Messiah*.
Concerto, I have an entire chapter later on this.

Handel borrowed lavishly from French classical drama, ancient Greek tragedy, the German Passion play, the English **masque,** and **full anthem;** no, not as in the national anthem for his oratorios. His important innovation was the use of the chorus.

 **Recommended Listening**

George Frideric Handel, "*The Arrival of the Queen of Sheba,*" from the oratorio *Solomon* (1749)
Solomon Budapest Strings
www.youtube.com/watch?v=-TGKJ9MgCOQ

Messiah is, of course, his most important oratorio. Everyone in Christendom knows that it's a fixture on many church and concert bills during the Christmas season and often during Easter since that's the season that Handel premiered it in Dublin, Ireland, in April 1742. It was billed then with what must be an oxymoron if there is one, "sacred entertainment." Remember, timing is everything.

Masque This is a festive event held in olden times with music and dancing, singing and acting, and a showy stage.

Full Anthem This is a song (then usually religious) that the entire choir sings.

Bach was regarded as one of the greatest organists of his day. He certainly did compose a rich and varied amount of music for the church, *St. Matthew Passion* (1727) and *St. John Passion* (1724). Both are regulars in the performance repertoire today, especially during religious seasons.

Vivaldi profoundly influenced Bach in his **preludes** and **fugues** for organ. His keyboard concertos, his two big chorales, Bach's *Well-Tempered Clavier* (1722), his English and French suites show the influence of French and Italian models. His *Goldberg Variations* (1741) are a joy to hear with their variety of notes and the sound they produce. The experts have always considered his music the near-complete package encompassing **harmony, counterpoint, melody, rhythm,** and inventiveness. And with good reason.

Counterpoint. This is crucial in classical music. If you play one melody simultaneously with another, they are playing counter to each other. This is a contrapuntal or, more commonly, counterpoint. Think of two dueling singers going at each other at the same time. All composers since then have genuflected to Bach for this; he is the absolute king of the hill of counterpoint.

Fugue It's literally a "chase" like to chase after each other. So certain parts or voices interchange at various points after each comes in.

Prelude is a short, open-ended composition musicians use to showcase their virtuosity.

Melody. This music moves in a straight line, one note after another.

Recommended Listening

Johann Sebastian Bach, *Brandenburg Concerto No. 2*
Freiburger Barockorchester
www.youtube.com/watch?v=3HSRIDtwsfM

✲ ✲ ✲ ✲ ✲

The times, though, were changing. The audiences wanted more varied sound and music. They especially wanted music with a lighter and clearer tone and a strong melody. The change ushered in a new era dubbed the **classical period,** which ran roughly from 1730 to 1820.

It was marked by greater variety, newer instruments, and a much bigger orchestra. One of the new instruments was the piano which replaced the harpsichord. Composers had a variety of forms they could use for their works the **sonata, trio, string quartet, quintet, concerto,** and the **symphony.** You'll learn more about these forms later.

Composers toured more, and with publishing increasingly more widespread, they could set their notes down with more specific and descriptive musical notation and distribute their written works more widely.

The hunger for even greater freedom and forms to express classical music ideas continued to grow. Composers sought to put more color, texture, and more vibrant, rich, and extended melody in their works. Most importantly, they wanted to express the range of human emotions in their works.

This ushered in a new period, the Romantic period from 1830 to 1910. This period spawned a new wave of works that were free-form **nocturnes, fantasias,** and **preludes** that were personal, expressive, and colorful. Meanwhile, the orchestras grew even bigger as more instruments continued to be added to produce a big, fulsome sound.

Nocturne. This is a short composition of a romantic or dreamy character suggestive of night, typically for piano.

Fantasia. This is a free-form work with a dreamy, mystical, magical sound and quality.

Prelude. This is an opening piece of music that can lead to successive movements or stand-alone work.

From the Concert Seat

The movie *Amadeus* was a stark example of Hollywood having great fun while taking lots of license with the life of a historical figure to pack the theaters. The irony is that Mozart's life was anything but that of the stereotyped dry, boring musician-composer. He wasn't poor, childlike with a high cackle voice, poisoned, or dumped into a pauper's grave as depicted in *Amadeus*.

He was a one-child showstopper and trickster with and on the piano, he gambled, shot pool, was a party goer, got cursed out by an archbishop, cavorted with an assortment of on-the-make musical hustlers, and ne'er do wells, got paid a lot of money at times for his music, and lived the high life with it. On his death bed, there was drama when a mysterious stranger commissioned him to write *The Requiem*. The stranger was a count who wanted to pawn off the piece as his own and make a killing off the forgery.

On December 14, 1791, his memorial service in Prague was a dramatic and moving affair in the streets with lots of boohoos from the thousands that flocked to it and music supplied by some of the city's best musicians. So, there are enough fun and drama in the real Amadeus to make a crackling good *Amadeus*.

One writer described the Romantic period as a period in which composers let loose with "powerful crescendos, pounding chords, and grand gestures. It was a period when composers gave free rein to their music's emotions, passions, and anxieties. It was big, often loud, and boisterous, and just as often soft, lush, and warmly melodic. No matter what the mood expressed, it was exciting music.

Recommended Listening

Anton Bruckner, *Symphony No. 4 in E flat Major "Romantic"*
Wiener Philharmoniker
www.youtube.com/watch?v=gcBg-tXn0fs

* * * * *

During the Romantic period, some composers went in a different direction. They boldly announced that they would tell a story with their work. The **tone poem** soon became the rage in the mid-19th Century. As the name suggests, it conveys a particular mood, feeling, and a composer's impression of what he saw in nature, everyday life, and the joys and agonies of human existence. It could be a nature scene, a personality, an event, a happening, a play, or a drama.

The composers spelled out their exact intent in the tone poem. It was written in one movement. It does not have the formal structure of a symphonic work, which is generally in four movements. I'll come back to structure and movements in my discussion of the symphony.

Beethoven kind of, sort of, kicked things off with his *Symphony No. 6 "Pastoral"* (1808). It's his homage to nature—the trees, the bird sounds, the weather (the storm and clearing), and his prayer of thanks at the end for the incredible beauty and power of nature. The instruments had a specific role in this type of work, and that was to express the mood of each scene depicted. So, the woodwinds and strings are the sound of calm and serenity. The timpani (drums) and trombones are the sound of the thunder of the coming storm.

Many composers weren't the only ones experimenting with new musically artistic forms in the 19th Century. Painters did too. They believed art should unapologetically express moods and feelings. In contrast, others thought that a painting should be purely the artist's impressions of how they saw and felt nature, a person, an event, or anything he captured on a canvas. The paintings of Cezanne, Monet, and Picasso, in particular, are rich in color and intensely engaging.

It didn't take long for some composers to pick up on this way of looking at life in their music. Some of them began to think of their music as paintings, impressionistic paintings. Suddenly we had yet another school of thought about what classical music should sound like in the Romantic era and even whether it should even be called classical music as such.

This time it was called **impressionism;** music with no particular program necessary, no rigid format, no big idea. The impressionist composer's works were just their impressions of a scene or something in nature or life.

Impressionism. Claude Debussy (France, 1862-1918), in his *Prelude to the Afternoon of a Faun* (1894), typifies the feeling that an impressionist composer wants the listener to hear. When asked what he sought to convey to the listener, he likened his music to a painting, "My prelude is really a sequence of mood paintings throughout in which the desire and drama of the faun move in the heat of the midday sun." Debussy's instruments to create that sense of movement provide added rich and color and texture to the work. It's as if the listener is looking at a painting and interpreting what's on canvas-in this case, the music—as they experience it.

His *Nocturnes* (1899) also express a subtle image of nightfall. Yet, it's his *La Mer* (1903-05), a major orchestral work filled with imagery, feeling, and the mood of the seascape, that made him the major proponent of impressionistic musical writing.

As with any other new trend that catches fire, other composers soon jumped on board. Here are some of the artists and their works by those who took a cue from Debussy. They blended musical imagery to capture the flavor and the color of a time, place, or storyline.

- Maurice Ravel (France, 1875-1937), no, not *Bolero*, but his *Daphnis et Chloé*, (1912)
- Isaac Albeniz (Spain, 1860-1909), *Iberia* (1892)
- Manuel de Falla (Spain, 1876-1946), *Nights in the Garden of Spain* (1915), and *The Three Corned Hat* (1919)
- Frederick Delius (England, 1862-1934), *A Summer Night on the River* (1911-12)
- Ottorino Respighi (Italy, 1879-1936), the *Pines of Rome* (1924), and *Fountains of Rome* (1928).

There was still more to come in innovation in the classical music world in the 19th Century. Johann Strauss, the junior (Austria, 1825-1899), took classical music out of the concert hall and put it on the dance floor. His music was the **waltz.** Although some of the classical purists frowned at the notion that anyone would call this anything like classical, it certainly caught the ear and the attention and admiration of the many traditional classical composers of that period, most notably Brahms.

Strauss admittedly had a much easier sell of the waltz than a standard four-movement symphony. The reason was simple. You could dance to it. It was music to dance to.

German composer Richard Strauss (1864-1949)

thought so much of the other Strauss, no relation, that he included Strauss's light-hearted rhythms and melodies like a waltz in his opera *Der Rosenkavalier* (1909-1910, The Cavalier of the Rose). They are exciting and fun listening and superbly rhythmic.

The best-known Johann Strauss waltzes, *The Blue Danube* (1866), *The Kaiser-Walzer,* (1889), and *Tales from the Vienna Woods* (1868), are standard numbers on concert bills. *The Blue Danube* even turned up in Kubrick's *2001: A Space Odyssey.*

Recommended Listening

Johann Strauss II, *The Blue Danube Waltz*
Vienna Philharmonic
www.youtube.com/watch?v=VSyJjycjr9I

* * * * *

By the mid-1800s, nationalism or national identity became the hot ticket item with many composers. They wove their country's national anthems, native dances, songs, folklore, and protest songs into their works. In particular, Peter Ilyich Tchaikovsky (1840-1893) incorporated Russian folk songs, melodies, and dances in his symphonies. Other composers also dug deep into their nation's culture and included native songs and dances, and melodies in their works. I'll talk more about this later.

Despite the new emphasis on national identity themes in their works, along with impressionism, the tone poem, and folk music and dance, the tried-and-true style of the old masters didn't die. They followed the rigid and standard classical movement forms faithfully. Camille Saint-Saens (France 1835-1921) wrote five brilliant and colorful piano concertos and three symphonies, notably *Symphony No. 3,* "The Organ Symphony."

French composer George Bizet of the opera *Carmen* fame (more on this later) stuck to the standard symphony format in his luxuriant, lively, and intensely youthful sounding *Symphony in C* (1855). Bizet wrote it at age 17. A student work closely copied in style his teacher, celebrated musician-composer, Charles Gounod's *Symphony in D Major* (1855).

The Russians didn't scrap the old four-movement symphony form either. Sergey Prokofiev (1891-1953), Igor Stravinsky (1882-1971), Nikolai Rimsky-Korsakov (1844-1908), and Dmitri Shostakovich (1906-1975) still wrote nearly all their symphonies, concertos, and chamber works in the old traditional four-movement forms. Prokofiev openly paid homage to Haydn's style and format with his *Symphony No. 1 "The Classical"* (1917).

The world-acclaimed Russian-born piano virtuoso and composer Sergei Rachmaninoff (1873-1943) eventually landed in America. He did not move one step from the traditional defined movement structure in his three symphonies and four piano concertos.

Prokofiev, in his seven symphonies, and Shostakovich, in his 15 symphonies, did not stray very far from the tried-and-true models of the past. The most cursory listen to Prokofiev's brooding, tense, yet stirring *Symphony No. 5* premiered in March 1945 on the verge of the Soviet Union's World War II triumph over Nazi Germany is in the standard four-movement symphonic form.

Russian composer Nikolai Rimsky-Korsakov (1844-1908) departed from the standard four-movement form in his best-known work *Scheherazade* (1888), a big-tone poemesque musical telling of the old *One Thousand and One Nights* collection of West and South Asian stories and folk tales compiled in Arabic. I'm not sure whether he thought of the work like a symphony. I know others have called it a symphony without the pretense of being a formal symphony. Symphony or no, it's always been another crowd-pleaser.

Many musicologists rank Stravinsky as a central transformative figure in classical music history. The ranking is much deserved. Stravinsky did what Beethoven did with his *Symphony No. 3, The Eroica Symphony.* He stood the music world on its head with his early path-breaking works, *The Firebird* (1910) and especially *The Rite of Spring* (1913).

They are primal, raw, driving, and intense. Yet they change up with moments of subtle quiescent that give a respite from the driving sound. It was a revolutionary sound a century ago when they were composed and even now. It was no surprise then that Stravinsky's, *The Rite of Spring* caused a scandal and bedlam at its premiere at Paris's Théâtre des Champs-Élysées on April 2, 1913. Stravinsky never stopped talking about that.

'Rite of Spring' still has power to shock audiences

By ROBERT M. ANDREWS
Associated Press Writer

WASHINGTON (AP) — Vaslav Nijinsky's "The Rite of Spring," the revolutionary ballet that provoked a riot at its Paris premiere 76 years ago, is showing the jaded world of the 1980s that it can still shock an audience.

When the Joffrey Ballet presented its revival of the long-lost Nijinsky masterpiece, set to Igor Stravinsky's jarringly primitive score, about 50 spectators stalked silently out of the Kennedy Center Opera House during Friday's opening-night performance.

was the result of seven years of painstaking detective work by Millicent Hodson, an American dance historian and choreographer, and Kenneth Archer, a British art historian.

After working with Nijinsky's former assistant, Marie Rambert, in London in the mid-1950s, Joffrey met Ms. Hodson, a graduate student at the University of California at Berkeley, in 1971 and encouraged her to pursue her research on Nijinsky and the Ballets Russes.

Starting in 1979 with only three black-and-white photographs of dancers from

Stravinsky also wrote more minor works, a concerto and two symphonies, such as the *Symphony in C* (1938-40). They are very much in the standard four-movement mode.

Antonin Dvorak (Czechoslovakia, 1841-1904) pretty much followed suit with his nine symphonies, and particularly his three major works, *Symphony No. 7*, his gift to a London audience as he put it, and *Symphony No. 8* (1889) and *Symphony No. 9*, "From the New World" (1893). These three symphonies are first-rate, major works that just about every orchestra pencils in on its program during their concert season. In this symphony, he drew heavily on African American spiritual and Native American rhythmic beats.

In England, Edward Elgar's (1857-1934) two symphonies—his *Symphony No. 1 in A Major* (1908) was used as the theme in the 1984 film, *Greystoke: The Legend of Tarzan*, and his *Pomp and Circumstance, No. 2* that generations of school kids have marched in time with at their graduation and his *Enigma Variations,* are the epitome of harmonious décor, though not precisely in the standard symphonic form. Likewise, Jean Sibelius's (Finland, 1865-1957) seven symphonies, especially his signature *Symphony No. 2,* adhere closely to the traditional old school models.

Recommended Listening

Antonin Dvorak, *Symphony No. 7 in D Minor*
Prague Symphony Orchestra
www.youtube.com/watch?v=3thKh93NEEU

Edward Elgar, *Symphony No. 1,* Op. 55
London Symphony Orchestra
www.youtube.com/watch?v=6SX9m2V9mbM

Sergei Prokofiev, *Symphony No. 5 in B Flat Major*
St. Petersburg Symphony Orchestra
www.youtube.com/watch?v=EaiXIdncA7M

Dvorak's *Czech Suite* (1879) and 16 *Slavonic Dances* (1876 and 1886), Prokofiev in his *Lieutenant Kije Suite* (1933), and Sibelius in *Lemminkäinen Suite (Four Legends from the Kalevala)* (1895) have been huge successes because of their emphasis on homegrown folk tales and themes. Sibelius took the patriotic banner to extraordinary lengths in his *Finlandia* (1898). He crowded it with folk and patriotic and religious themes in part to thumb his nose at the rule of Czarist Russia over Finland (it was a duchy of Russia before 1917).

Another Russian composer, Dimitri Shostakovich (1906-1975), also gave nods to Russian and Jewish folk music. However, they were still solid classicists in that they structured their symphonies in the traditional movement form.

Recommended Listening

Dimitri Shostakovich, *Symphony No. 11 in G Minor 'The Year 1905,"*
Mariinsky Theatre Orchestra
www.youtube.com/watch?v=wW5USVKVAx4

Composers in the United States in the 1920s and 1930s also began incorporating jazz and Americana themes in their works. George Gershwin's landmark *Rhapsody in Blue* (1924) piano concerto drew heavily on jazz rhythms.

But jazz aside, Gershwin's piano concertos that did not radically depart from the standard movement format. Aaron Copland paid tribute to American folk music songs and themes in his ballet, *Appalachian Spring* (1944). However, Copland's three symphonies closely followed the traditional symphonic forms.

African American composer William Grant Still's (1897-1978) wildly popular *Symphony No.1 in A-flat Major* (1930) known as the *"Afro-American Symphony"* is written in the standard four-movement form.

Florence Price (1887-1953) wrote her famed *Piano Concerto in D Minor* (1934) in the traditional three-movement form.

Recommended Listening

Florence Price, *Piano Concerto in D Minor*
Lawrence Symphony Orchestra
www.youtube.com/watch?v=HODqVHYDVDg

George Gershwin, *Rhapsody in Blue*
Royal Philharmonic Orchestra
www.youtube.com/watch?v=eFHdRkeEnpM

Aaron Copland, *Symphony No. 3*
New York Philharmonic Orchestra
www.youtube.com/watch?v=pfqCo_vuMsI

The modernism these composers brought to classical music from 1890 to 1930 marked an era when many composers rejected the older, established styles of classical music, such as traditional tonality, melody, instrumentation, and structure. I'll explain and discuss these musical terms and concepts later.

During these varied periods, the many changes in classical music—baroque, classical, romantic, and then modernism—deeply influenced each new crop of composers. They borrowed from the previous periods in the types of instruments used, the changing forms they wrote in, and the changing structures of their works. They extended, expanded, experimented with, and retooled the models from each period to redefine the shape of classical music.

2

The Symphony

*"A symphony must be like the world.
It must embrace everything."*
—Gustav Mahler

"Composing is like driving down a foggy road toward a house. Slowly you see more details of the house—the colors of the slates and bricks, the shape of the windows. The notes are the bricks and the mortar of the house." This is how Britten once described the often-rigorous task of composing. I can say the same when dissecting classical music, notably the twin centerpiece of the music, the symphony. The other is opera. I'll get to that soon.

I'll start with my introduction to classical music. In my first year in college, I had to take a required music appreciation course. I dreaded it. I just did not want to sit in class for an hour and listen to stodgy music from a bunch of long-dead Europeans. But it was a requirement, so I had little choice but to endure the pain.

Then something happened. The instructor played a work that didn't sound too bad. A few minutes into it, he stopped and said, "This is a symphony." He continued for a few more minutes. He stopped it. He said this is the **andante.** For the next half hour or so, he stopped and started the work. This is the **allegro.** This is the **scherzo.** This is the **minuet.** This is a **scale.** This is a **chord.** This is a **note.** This is a **major key.** This is a **minor key.** Don't panic; I'll explain what they all are as we move along.

Finally, he played most of the symphony in its entirety without interruption. It was the Beethoven *Symphony No. 7* (1811-1812). This was all a very remote foreign language to me. I didn't then connect the terminology with the music. I did, though, connect the sound. It sounded powerful even with my non-understanding of what I heard, let alone what the terms meant.

Major and Minor Keys. This is the root or sometimes called home chord in which a composer chooses to write their work. It's the root of harmony in a work. It could be D Minor A Major, E Minor B Major, etc.

Recommended Listening

Ludwig van Beethoven, *Symphony No 7 in A Major* Concertgebouw Orchestra of Amsterdam
https://www.youtube.com/watch?v=5ol_DArX3CI

* * * * *

No matter how much, or rather how little one knows about classical music, most have heard the word symphony. Gustav Mahler (1860-1911) was enthralled with its sweep and scope. As you see from his quote, he claimed that it embraced everything. Well, maybe not quite everything. However, it's a word that has seeped into much of our everyday conversation. Such as It's a symphony of words. It's a symphony of life. It's a symphony of happiness. In classical music, a symphony always evokes a large, even momentous sound.

The word symphony, like so many other words and terms in classical music, was handed down to us from the Italians or the Greeks. It means "agreement or concord of sound." Many of the world's top orchestras have ensured that audiences know that they are symphony orchestras. There is the London Symphony Orchestra, the Boston Symphony Orchestra, the St. Louis Symphony, the Houston Symphony, Miami's New World Symphony, and the Vancouver Symphony Orchestra, to name a very few.

The basic definition of a symphony is a somewhat lengthy musical work played by an orchestra. The orchestra can have almost any number of instruments. They are arranged in sections—woodwinds, the brass, the percussions, and the strings. Here's the list of the instruments in each section:

- Strings: Violin, Viola, Cello, and Double Bass
- Woodwinds: Flute, Piccolo, Oboe, Bassoon, Clarinet, Bass clarinet, English Horn, Contrabassoon, and Saxophone
- Brass: Trumpet, Trombone, French Horn, Tuba,
- Percussion: Snare Drum, Timpani, Triangle, Bass Drum, Cymbal, Piano, Gong, and Vibraphone

They are in sections for a simple reason. They produce different sounds, and they must be coordinated with the other sections. If not, it would be a musical mish-mash.

* * * * *

In the early years of classical music, before the middle of the 1700s, symphonies did not have the one feature that is the trademark of the symphony. Usually, the musicians were led by a violinist who waved his bow, shifted his eyes head, and nodded at the various players to keep them on track. That's the conductor.

By the early 1800s, symphonic orchestras had grown much more extensive. They now needed someone out front to serve as a traffic cop. The conductor emerged. Their job was to direct, coordinate, and blend the sounds and instruments. They must make sure they are all playing on the same page, whatever work they are playing. Let's fine-tune that. They set the beat or tempo or timing. That's the speed the piece is played at. They then tease out the musical nuances and emphasize the particular musical instruments.

They usually do that with a baton. However, some conductors scrap the baton and use just their hands. The conductor goes the whole body. He uses hand, facial and body gestures to keep the flow of the music going. They point and look at one or more of the musicians. If you are seated close to the orchestra, you can hear the conductor chatting at times with the orchestra.

Before leaving the conductor, it's worth noting a variation on the adage the more things change, the more they can stay the same. Some orchestras still dispense with a conductor. Some of the world's leading orchestras have gone the conductor-less route: The Orpheus Chamber Orchestra, the Prague Chamber Orchestra, the Amsterdam Sinfonietta, the New Century Chamber Orchestra, the East Coast Chamber Orchestra, and the Advent Chamber Orchestra are conductor less.

Starting in the early nineteenth century, symphonies had parts to them. Parts didn't quite fit the sense of what a symphony was. In time parts became known as movements.

Movement. This is a self-contained part of a musical composition or musical form. You'll see and hear a symphony referred to as "first movement," "second movement," and so on.

The movements fittingly were given names—all of which were in Italian. The most common are the alle**gro, andante, tempo di marcia, andante maestoso, larghetto-allegretto.** The first movement is usually fast, the second one is slow, the third is medium, and the fourth movement is fast. The idea is to keep the music varied and thus interesting. Speed or tempo is the key to ensuring that. The movements have other names, and I have listed them below with their meanings.

Allegro is a tempo marking for classical music. It says that the music is to be played moderately fast.

Adagio is a tempo (speed) marking indicating that music is to be played slowly or a composition intended to be played in this manner.

Minuet and **trio** is a tempo marking indicating that the music is played and danced.

Rondo form and **sonata** form is a tempo marking indicating the music is to be played with the theme repeated with variations on that theme or even new themes stuck in between. It is divided into sections.

* * * * *

Let's continue with the movements.

The **first movement** was almost always fast. Composers knew they had to hit the ground running and get the audience's attention. So, what better way to do that than with an upbeat tempo.

The **second movement** slows down, sometimes way down.

The **third movement** is generally moderately paced. It's not too fast, not too slow. Often it is a minuet. That was the dance of the royal court in the 19th century. The minuet was/is dancelike.

The **fourth movement** hits speed dial. It barrels along at an up-tempo pace. The composer wants to bring the audience to their feet. Or, at the least, give them a strong close and something to remember. The four movements of arguably the most popular and most frequently played of all symphonies are here. Why, because it starts with that "da-

da-da-*dum.*" It's Beethoven's *Symphony No. 5* (1808).

Those opening notes have been used in films, TV shows, and commercials. It got global notoriety when it became the symbol for victory during World War II because the notes matched the rhythm of the letter V in Morse Code (short-short-short-long).

Beethoven's Symphony No. 5
First movement: Allegro con brio (8:20)
Second movement: Andante con moto (9:59)
Third movement: Scherzo. Allegro (5:36)
Fourth movement: Allegro (11:47)

A few more prominent symphonic composers didn't just stop with instrumental music. They added voice, either individual voices and a chorus, or both to their works. Beethoven's *Symphony No. 9* (1822-1824), best known as the *"Choral Symphony"* because its closing movement contains the rousing "Ode to Joy," is by far the best example.

* * * * *

In several of his works, particularly *Symphony No. 2, "The Resurrection,"* Mahler wrapped nearly the entire symphony around a chorus and solo voices.

What exactly are sections? This is an excellent time to introduce a few more commonly used musical terms. There is an **introduction.** That's simply the opening theme. There is an **exposition.** That presents the main them. That is set in a **key.** It could be a major key. Remember, the purpose of the major key is to create sound loud or forceful. If it's in a minor key, the sound is soft and demurring. This, in turn, creates the desired mood.

Then there is the **development.** That is a repeat of the theme or themes in a new way with a unique sound. The sound is **harmony** or **texture.** A work would be pretty dull listening without varying the theme or presenting it differently. This is what creates a distinctive sound.

An important point to remember when listening to the symphony is that these terms represent themes and how they are presented to the listener. If you listen closely, you will hear the theme or themes repeated in varied forms and with assorted instruments during the performance of the work.

There's one more term to be familiar with in describing the themes.

That's **recapitulation.** The theme or themes are repeated.

From the Concert Seat

The Orpheus Chamber Orchestra, the Prague Chamber Orchestra, the Amsterdam Sinfonietta, the

New Century Chamber Orchestra, the East Coast Chamber Orchestra, and the Advent Chamber Orchestra are well known and internationally acclaimed. They have one thing in common—no conductor. Most 17th and into the 18th Century orchestras didn't have a conductor. That changed in the 19th century when the conductor became a big name. The band's leader then was the concertmaster or the continuo player, generally the harpsichordist that led the orchestra with a few head nods and waves of the hand. Almost no one knew his name.

So how suddenly did one man get to be the big money guy, the prima donna who grabs the glory and fame, is wined and dined endlessly, and is considered an orchestra's single biggest asset? Well, from the technical, leadership, and aesthetic view, the conductor's job is to set the right tempo (beat) the timing, tease out the musical nuances, emphasize key musical elements, and in general, bring unity and coherence to the orchestra. They do that through their hand, facial, and body gestures nuances and by controlling the flow of the sound. Since dozens of musicians wailing away, but only one conductor, somebody has to lead.

Now I'll bring in science to try to answer that question. Researchers at the University of Maryland in 2014 conducted a study that used infrared lights to measure the musicians of the orchestra's reactions to the conductor. The conclusion: "What we found is the more the influence of the conductor to the players, the more aesthetic—aesthetically pleasing the music was overall."

Leave it to science, then to confirm the value of at least one member of an orchestra. And we certainly know that the member in question, the conductor, wouldn't dispute their value, no matter how many questions may be asked about that value.

The man widely considered the father of the symphonic work was the Austrian court composer Franz Joseph Haydn. (1737-1806) Haydn wrote at least 106 symphonies over 36 years. He gets prime credit for expanding the symphony from three movements to four movements.

More movements called for more instruments. Many of them were new to the scene. This added greater length to a work. During the early 1800s, symphonies became longer and longer. An early Haydn and Wolfgang Amadeus Mozart (1756-1791) work were three movements. It would typically last around 20 minutes. With the added fourth movement and more instruments, symphonies now stretched out in some cases to 30 minutes or more.

Recommended Listening

Wolfgang Amadeus Mozart, *Symphony No. 41 C Major,* *"The Jupiter"*
Berliner Philharmoniker
www.youtube.com/watch?v=oHuhATcs99E

* * * * *

The flutes, oboes, clarinets and bassoons, a pair of horns, and timpani are the instruments that soon became fixtures in an orchestra. Often, there was a harpsichord (the forerunner to the piano), a small piano characteristic of Bach's time in the late 1600s and early 1700s.

By the early 1800s, the four-movement symphony, as noted, had become the gold standard structure for most symphonies. Composers also became sticklers for marking their notes, the tempo they wanted the piece played at, and the keys they wanted them played in.

Once the four-movement symphony firmly took hold, the prominent composers of the nineteenth century stayed within its rigid structure. Beethoven wrote nine symphonies, Brahms wrote four symphonies, Robert Schumann (1810-1856) wrote four symphonies, Felix Mendelssohn (1809-1847) wrote five major symphonies. Franz Schubert (1797-1828) wrote nine symphonies. Peter Tchaikovsky wrote six major symphonies. They are all four-movement works.

A few composers had other ideas about what a symphony should sound and even look like. They wanted to tell a story with their symphonies or other musical works. It might be a story of lost love, such as Berlioz's *Symphony Fantastique* (1830). I'll talk more about this work later.

It might be a story based on myths and legends. Wagner set his operas with a generous amount of instrumental music that sounded like mini symphonic works in structure. Franz Liszt's best known of his tone poems *Les Preludes* (1849), attained storybook movieland fame as the theme for the 1930s sci-fi adventure series *Flash Gordon* and parts of it in the *Lone Ranger* radio series in the 1940s. Nearly all Richard Strauss's (1864-1949) significant works had names, were based on fables. And they had heroic storylines to go with it.

- *Don Juan*
- *Ein Heldenleben (A Hero's Life)*
- *Also Sprach Zarathustra*
- *Till Eulenspiegel's Merry Pranks*
- *An Alpine Symphony*

Since they had a name and a story to tell, they called them program music. They were a bit more than just storyline music. They had a specific tone, and they were likened to poems. So, they were given the formal name, **tone poem.** I'll cover this more later. **Tone Poem** is a one-movement orchestral work that tells a story.

The traditional symphony, however, was not dead. Sir Edward Elgar and Mahler wrote stupendous symphonies in length, the number of instruments, and vocalists. Mahler's *Symphony No. 8* in E-flat Major was composed in 1906 and is nicknamed the *"Symphony of a Thousand"* because of the many voices required to perform it.

The symphony in its four-movement form continued to reign supreme in classical music in the mid to late 1800s. Few composed masterworks better in the four-movement form than the composer who I've heard almost as much as Beethoven. That's Peter Ilyich Tchaikovsky (1840-93). He is much closer to being an old-school classic symphony composer. However, being the innovator he was, he added a new dimension to his six numbered symphonies. He borrowed heavily from traditional Russian folk themes and embedded them in his symphonies.

The best example is his *Symphony No. 2, "The Little Russian"* (1872). This is a musical tribute to Ukrainian folk music at the time. The Ukraine then was known as "Little Russia." He uses a French horn in the first movement to solo based on the Ukrainian folk song "Down by Mother Volga." He repeats this theme at different points through the symphony. The rest of the symphony strictly conforms to the standard four-movement work: slow (andante) tempo picks up (allegro) and an explosive fourth movement in part based on another Ukrainian folk tune, "The Crane."

Tchaikovsky wasn't delighted with the work and made several revisions. His instructions to his publisher tell us much about what a composer seeks in a finished four-movement symphony, "1. I have composed the first movement afresh, leaving only the introduction and coda in their previous form. 2. I have rescored the second movement. 3. I've altered the third movement, shortening and rescoring it. 4. I've shortened the finale and rescored it."

His prodigious output of symphonies, piano and violin concertos, ballets, and numerous small chamber works include a lot of Russian folk music and Russian life. His symphonies are second to none among the old masters regarding sheer, raw, almost animalistic power, energy, and passion in the music. His symphonies best represent the big, explosive sound in a symphonic work.

Recommended Listening

Peter Ilich Tchaikovsky, *Symphony No. 2 in C Minor "Little Russian"*
Stanford Summer Symphony Orchestra
www.youtube.com/watch?v=WfAyIL8fb5I

Peter Ilich Tchaikovsky, *Symphony No. 5 in E Minor,* Op. 64
Russian State Symphony Orchestra
www.youtube.com/watch?v=8pmdlgKalyQ

Tchaikovsky wasn't the only old school composer in the north of Europe near the turn of the twentieth century to continue to write in the standard symphonic form. Finnish composer Jean Sibelius in his *Symphony No. 2 in D Major,* retained the old classical structured form even when he didn't formally separate the varied movements.

🎧 Recommended Listening

Jean Sibelius, *Symphony No. 2 in D Major*
Iceland Symphony Orchestra
www.youtube.com/watch?v=Z6iNaFWV3tc

* * * * *

Mahler, then, was on to something when he said the symphony should embrace the world. Consider all the multiple elements that go in a symphony, the dozens of instruments, the dozens of musicians playing them, lots of notes, lots of ideas, and lots of themes. You know that composers are trying to convey a world of musical power, wonder, and adventure to the listener.

The symphony is the one part of classical music that, in name, most people know of and associate with classical music. Mahler, though, didn't have the only word about the symphony. Leonard Bernstein had another take on what the orchestra should be about.

"I am not interested in having an orchestra sound like itself. I want to sound it as the composer."

Bernstein left little doubt that the composer should have the final word on what the orchestra and, by extension, the symphony should be about. There it is. Mahler and Bernstein's take on the symphony. They are both right in their way. It can encompass the world and the individual.

3

The Concerto

"I have in accordance with Your Highness's most gracious orders taken the liberty of rendering my most humble duty to Your Royal Highness with the present Concertos, which I have adapted to several instruments."

The quote is from a letter Johann Sebastian Bach wrote in 1721 to Christian Ludwig (1677-1734), the Margrave of Brandenburg-Schwedt (often referred to as the Earl of Brandenburg),

This letter has been read and cited countless times in part and in its entirety down not through the years but the centuries. It has been laughed at, joked about, and derided. But mostly, it has made heads shake. They shake their heads because here is the great Bach shamelessly groveling in the letter to a royal personage about the new set of six concertos he had written.

Bach wrote the concertos and the letter hoping that the Margrave would be so impressed with them that he would give him a job at court. The job was a kind of court musical director or Kapellmeister in German.

* * * * *

The custom in the 18th century and before was that if a composer and musician wanted to get any place in the classical music business, he had to find a wealthy patron. Almost always, this was a king, emperor, royal personage, or in the church, the cardinal or archbishop. They had the money, the prestige, and could afford to employ musicians.

Bach's letter didn't do a darn thing for him. He didn't get the job. The concertos meant nothing to the Margrave. As Bach scholars point out, he tossed them aside and almost certainly never listened to a note of any of the six. They languished in obscurity for a century after Bach's death in 1750. They were unearthed and published in 1850.

Though it took a century after he was gone for the world to discover Bach's concertos, the Margrave of Brandenburg did give the world a name to Bach's concertos:

"*Brandenburg.*" They have been the platinum standard for concertos ever since.

What is the **concerto,** and how does it differ from a symphony? The short answer is it does, and it doesn't differ. The word "concerto" is Italian. It means "agreeing" or "playing together." Before that, its Latin root was concerto, Latin verb concertare. This meant a competition or battle.

A concerto is performed with a symphony orchestra. The notes that the orchestra plays are the symphony's **score.** At the conductor's side and in front of the orchestra is a solo performer. They are more likely than not to play the violin or the piano. The orchestra will play alone a part of the composition. The soloists will play alone for part of the composition. Then there will be times when both play together. Some liken the concerto to a duel. More charitably, it is an interplay between the orchestra and the soloist and their instrument.

Score. The notes, the parts for different instruments, and various notions about the tempo on pages.

* * * * *

There practically isn't an instrument in creation that a concerto hasn't been written for. It was only a matter of time before a composer would pull one of the instruments out of the orchestra and write music for an artist to play it with and apart from the orchestra. When that happened, the concerto was born. The most common are—violin concerto, piano concerto, cello concerto, flute concerto, clarinet concerto, harp concerto, guitar concerto, or even a tuba or organ concerto, a accordion concerto, and a harmonica concerto.

Most notably Brahms, Beethoven, and Mozart, some composers weren't satisfied with just basing their concerto on one instrument. They wrote concertos for multiple instruments, two and even three pianos.

Recommended Listening

Ludwig van Beethoven, *Concerto for Piano, Violin, Cello and Orchestra, "Triple Concerto,"* Op. 56
La Orquesta Sinfónica de Galicia
www.youtube.com/watch?v=hZZaztTNsEc

Johannes Brahms, *Double Concerto for Violin, Cello, and Orchestra in A Minor*
McGill Symphony Orchestra
www.youtube.com/watch?v=Vo4VRVyRuHw

The Concerto

> **From the Concert Seat**
>
> Though I've heard it played many times by orchestras and soloists, I purposely didn't spotlight Rachmaninoff's crowd favorite, *Rhapsody on a Theme of Paganini* (1934), here. It is undeniably a moving, beautiful, full-throated work. Still, I have not mentioned it above precisely because it's probably the one work that is recognizable by many who couldn't care less about classical music. In other words, it sells itself as a showpiece work.

In the late 18th and 19th centuries, the concerto came into its own in the classical music world. The symphonies at first had three movements. Later they increased to four movements. The concerto, like the symphony, at first also were usually three-movement works. The three movements, also like the symphony, were in the temp of fast-slow-fast. This was not set in stone. In later years there were famed concertos that started slowly. Some concertos start with an agonizingly slow opening. There was much flexibility.

Recommended Listening

Sergei Rachmaninoff, *Piano Concerto No. 2*
Evgeny Kissin, Piano
Orchestre Philharmonique de Radio France
www.youtube.com/watch?v=l4zkc7KEvYM

The concerto is a showpiece work for the individual soloist and their instrument. The best-known and the not-so-best-known composers all wrote concertos. In many cases, they wrote the work for a musician they were friends with and respected their playing of the chosen instrument. Often that artist was themselves. They would premier a new concerto with themselves at the keyboard.

Mozart and Beethoven were topflight pianists. So piano concertos gave them the chance to showcase their playing and the work. It killed three birds with one stone. It brought them more performance money, audience popularity, and a vehicle to premier their composition. Many wrote their **cadenzas** to drive the point home to audiences about their virtuosity, even showiness, on the instrument.

Cadenza is Italian. It means cadence. A cadenza can be written out or just improvised depending on the performer's mood at the moment. It can be fast or slow. They can take off in any musical flight of fancy that suits them. The flight can last for a few seconds or several minutes. There is no actual time constraint. While they play to their musical heart's content, the conductor stands stark still. The orchestra musicians sit stark still. It's a waiting game. When the soloist runs out of steam, all swing back into action and carry the piece forward.

The Concerto

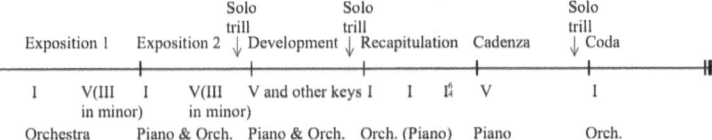

This graphic shows how the composition is structured with the orchestra-piano and orchestra and the cadenza.

As mentioned previously, the orchestra continued to grow from the mid-1750s on. The soloist now faced and had to complement their playing with more instruments in the orchestra. Composers also had to adjust. They now had the instruments to create even bigger, lusher, more expansive works. This change also posed a more significant challenge for the soloist. They had to get better and more proficient. There were complaints. Some musicians couldn't handle the technical demands of the new works and didn't even bother to try their hand at these works.

The difficulty some musicians had with some of the more complex works was the subject of a Hollywood movie, *Shine* (1996), starring Geoffrey Rush as the musically challenged pianist determined to master a work. The work that stumped him in the film and many other real-life soloists for a time was the Rachmaninoff *Piano Concerto No. 3*.

However, younger, more skilled players came on the scene who were up to the challenge in time. The new crop of soloists now handled some of the previously deemed unplayable works with ease. P. S. Rush won the Academy

Award for his performance. Should he and we thank Rachmaninoff for that accolade?

* * * * *

I have seen many great virtuoso pianists in concerts. They all have their way of doing things on stage. They can thank one composer for making stage presence as part of a solo performance as the playing itself. Yet they share one commonality: They know all eyes in the audience are glued on them, and they are the show.

Franz Liszt (Germany, 1811-86) pioneered the piano recital and other instruments. He brought audacious, showy, and dazzling virtuosity to his piano performances, complete with hair flying, arms waving, and head rocking back and forth before head-banging was in style. In one way or another, many pianists try to emulate some or all of that in their performances.

Musicologists love to label Liszt as the first true rock star, especially since women mobbed the stage to touch and ogle him while he played a work for all it was worth. Yes, Hans Christian Anderson, the famed fabler himself, attended one of his concerts in 1840 and was thoroughly awed by him. Said the storyteller: "The instrument appeared to be changed into a whole orchestra, and when he finished playing, the flowers rained down on him."

Beethoven's *Piano Concerto No. 5, "The Emperor"* (1809-11), is a big, bold, rangy work that captures the passion and verve of the mature Beethoven. Beethoven went further and used powerful contrasts to broaden the piano's expressive range. Forget tickling the ivories; he pounded them! Unfortunately, almost certainly because of his advancing deafness, this was the one work he did not perform at its premiere. The pity because this was his most remarkable and last piano concerto, which he could have used to showpiece his prodigious piano virtuosity.

The concerto has a grand opening, a dreamy Mozart-like second movement, and a blazing finish. It never fails to stir joy and sentimentality in many alternately. An interesting side note on its nickname, *"The Emperor"*: Like most of the nicknames of a grand, new piece by a major composer, this was not Beethoven's doing. His English publisher, Johann Baptist Cramer, sniffed more dollars in having a catchy nickname befitting its grandeur, rather than simply calling it *Piano Concerto No. 5*.

* * * * *

Let's turn back to Bach and the *Brandenburg Concertos*. The elements that make up these concertos in one form or another for the next three centuries were firmly established as the template for the concerto form.

The six *Brandenburgs* feature a variety of instruments in the orchestras. They are:

Concerto No. 1	• natural horns
Concerto No. 2	• trumpet
	• recorder
	• oboe
	• violin
Concerto No. 3	• 3 violins
	• 3 violas
	• 3 cellos and harpsichord
Concerto No. 4	• 2 recorders
	• violin
Concerto No. 5	• flute
	• violin
	• harpsichord

Concerto No. 6
- 2 violas
- 2 violas da gamba
- cello
- violone
- harpsichord

The *Brandenburg Concerto No. 1* is the only one of the six that departs from the rule. It has four movements. Fast (allegro) slow (adagio) fast (allegro) and minuet. The others are three-movement works. They were very short. The reason is twofold. There were fewer instruments in an orchestra in the 1700s. There were fewer musicians to play them. The *Brandenburgs* required fewer than 20 in all.

I chose this one because it is a four-movement work and to show the order of a four-movement work.

Brandenburg Concerto No. 1
First movement: Allegro (4:36)
Second movement: Adagio (4:42)
Third movement: Allegro (4:33)
Fourth movement:
Menuet; Trio 1; Polacca; Trio 2 (8:00)

Bach did something else that became and remains a fairly common practice for composers. He reworked some of his works. This was particularly true with concertos. They'd go through many drafts. They'd rearrange the parts, the instruments (adding and subtracting instruments from the orchestra), and vary the length by dropping or adding movements. Often, they'd make the changes after the work was premiered.

They were motivated to change because they weren't satisfied with the sound. Or the audiences and the critics panned it or out and out trashed it. Nothing was sacred or written in stone in the writing of a classical music piece.

* * * * *

There is no evidence that Bach changed things around in the Brandenburgs because of any negative blowback. He was just simply the consummate innovator with instruments and with sound. He wanted to get them right to his satisfaction.

A final note. The *Brandenburg No. 1* had the unique distinction of making a space journey. The first movement of this concerto is part of an array of sounds compiled on the Voyager Golden Record. It was packed away and played on two Voyager probes. It has also been used as a theme for a couple of popular TV programs and arranged for rock and electronic music pieces.

🎧 Recommended Listening

J. S. Bach in Rock
www.youtube.com/watch?v=5atiMihJJ2c

Concertos have proven especially popular classical works for another reason. They are true entertainment. As I noted earlier, the soloist is right in front of the audience, shifting, nodding, and sometimes elevating from their piano seat. Then there are the hands. The soloists' hands are riveting on the piano or violin. This draws attention and creates emotionally pleasing identification. Mozart certainly understood the entertainment value of concertos. He wrote a lot of them (27). Here's what he had to say about three of them that he wrote back-to-back in a letter to his father in the fall of 1782:

> "These concertos [Nos. 11, 12, and 13] are a happy medium between easy and difficult; they are brilliant, pleasing to the ear, and natural, without being vapid. There are passages here and there from which the connoisseurs alone can derive satisfaction, but these passages are written so that the less learned cannot fail to be pleased, though without knowing why.... The golden mean of truth in all things is no longer either known or appreciated. In order to win applause, one must write stuff which is so inane that a coachman could sing it, or so unintelligible that it pleases precisely because no sensible man can understand it."

I'll try to bring some understanding to it in my section on the soloist.

Mozart aimed to please an audience. Yes, the art is abundantly there, and all the musical elements of a concerto are there in abundance. But in the end, concertos are written to entertain. The concerto has more than proven its value on this score. The concerto was the second of the big three of classical music. The third is opera. Let's turn to it.

4

The Opera

> "Our mistake, you see, was to write interminable large operas, which had to fill an entire evening. And now along comes someone with a one or two-act opera without all that pompous nonsense— that was a happy reform."
> —Giuseppe Verdi

Verdi's point, though, is well taken about opera. There are almost as many lovers of it as loathers of it. That's not surprising. Unlike the symphony and concerto, opera tells a story, is staged, and there's lots of varied singing. Verdi can say that because his trend-setting operas were never considered pompous, let alone nonsense, by any opera lover.

The textbook definition of **opera** is it's a drama set to music. Just about everything is sung. So, if one doesn't like dramas, then a drama with a song isn't going to thrill that person either. Yet, opera is one of the oldest forms of music in the classical music world. It is very much Italian in its origins.

Let's familiarize ourselves with the structure and the standard terms of opera.

The Italian word opera means "work." In the sense of labor performed and the result the work produces. The Italian word derives from the Latin word *opera,* which is a singular noun meaning "work." It's also the plural of the Latin noun **opus,** which is what composers term their works.

Opera is performed on a stage. It generally opens with an **overture.** This is purely an instrumental opening the orchestra plays. Often, the overture has tunes that appear again in some form or another during the staging. The overture is not incidental or an afterthought to the main action on the stage. Opera composers put a lot into the overture to rev up the audience, grab attention, and add musical drama to the production.

Next, there's the **chorus.** A chorus is a group of singers who are often seen and heard in crowd scenes.

Operas are divided into acts. They may be a one-act production, or they can go big and stretch the action out to five acts. A staple in opera and what many who have watched any part of an opera know is that there is a star who takes center stage—the solo performer. The star sings what's called **arias.** This is a solo part with lyrics and orchestral accompaniment.

In the early operas in the 17th century, the singing would be broken up by what is known as a recitative. It goes like this. The lead singer sings the aria. Then they would mouth the storyline as a dialogue with a character or just as a monologue. To liven things up in the opera, some operas tossed in dances. The French, in particular, loved to have the players at times dancing around on stage.

From the Concert Seat

There was a kind of perverse gender poetic justice on the opera stage early. Women were strictly forbidden to sing any high pitch alto and soprano roles. But it would look and sound a little peculiar with the only voices and sounds heard sung on stage in the more resounding male tenor and bass voices. Opera guys found a way around it. They had men sing the high range parts. There was one small problem, the boys eventually became men, and their voices changed, like getting deeper.

The solution was painfully simple. I use the word painfully knowingly. They castrated the boys before puberty to be opera singers. They were called the castrati. That stopped nature in its tracks, and in physiological terms, a boy's larynx was frozen in its developmental tracks like, well, that of a boy.

In time and presumably with more enlightenment with the times, as well as the sudden discovery that women could sing as alto and sopranos, the practice mercifully ended. Fittingly enough, it happened in the land of opera. Italy made castration for singing anyway, illegal in 1870.

* * * * *

The orchestra has a fascinating history. In the early 1700s, operas used just a tiny handful of instruments, almost all string instruments. They did not accompany the singers. That was done with individual instruments like a lute or a harpsichord, the small piano of that era.

The audience heard the orchestra only at the beginning of the production playing the opening overture. It also might come in when a song ended. The music was used as a filler. It was more a relaxed, musical interlude. Opera composers soon figured out that if they had the instruments, why not use them and not separate them from the action.

Orchestral music was gradually integrated into the production, backing up the singers and the chorus.

Operatic orchestras in the later 1800s grew larger; more instruments, more percussions (bass drum, cymbals, snare drum), and more players. The enlarged orchestras produced crashing sounds if it was a battle, fight, or action scene. If it were a starry-eyed love scene, they'd switch gears and provide a beautifully lush, romantic sound.

The conductor of a large orchestra faced new challenges. He had to direct the singers on stage as well as the orchestra. A skilled conductor was indispensable to ensure that the production did not sink into a music and vocal-free for all.

By the mid-1800s, operas had varied forms.

Grand Opera. It's big and nothing but music. It's not to be confused with the Grand Ole Opry—the world-famous radio broadcast out of Nashville, Tennessee, that has been the musical Bible of bluegrass, Americana, folk, and gospel music for decades.

Opéra Bouffe. This is a comic opera. There are many wisecracks, gags, buffoonery, and slapstick action in this one. The point is to get you laughing.

Opéra Comique. In contrast to the Grand Opera, it has lots of chatter. The name comic doesn't do justice to this. It may be a tragedy. A lot of opera is based on tragedy.

Not all operas are extensive, lengthy, splashy affairs. There is a mini version, the **operetta.** It's a relatively short opera that quickly gets in and out of the action. It's almost always light, amusing, and airy.

The Italians and the French were opera pioneers and had their unique styles. However, the Germans brought in another opera form. It's called **singspiel**. It's full of fantasy themes and lots of dialogue between the songs. Some of Richard Wagner's (1813-1883) operas fit into this category.

However, Mozart's most beloved and ranked by many as his best opera, *The Magic Flute* (1791), is most often cited as an example of the singspiel. The story is packed with lots of magical imagery and fantasy. There are lots of spoken words in between the songs.

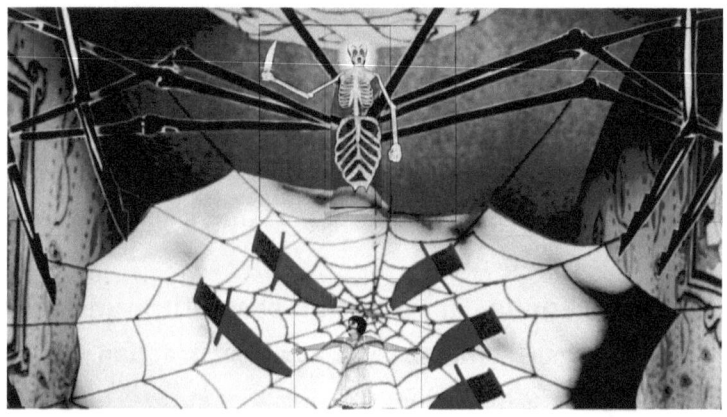

From the Concert Seat

This is the graphic promotion for the Houston Grand Opera's rendition of *The Magic Flute,* which opened in February 2022 in Houston. "It just plays so well, just as a piece of music theater," says Erik Friedman, Houston Grand opera's revival director. This happened to be Houston. But I can tell you there's probably not a place somewhere on the globe 200 plus years after Mozart wrote the opera that it isn't playing somewhere. The Houston production is another testament to its enduring magic and mystery.

* * * * *

What would opera be without the singer? Not just any old singer singing any old song, but beautiful, captivating singing. It would be like trying to play football without a ball without that. There's a term for this kind of singing. It's called **bel canto,** translated: beautiful voice.

The singer showcases their technique, style, and tone, giving full rein to their vocal range, flexibility, agility, and command of melodies. That's a lot to pack into the human voice. But that's a requirement of opera, that is, if the **diva** or **divo** wants to keep their audience spellbound.

Diva. This is the Latin word for a goddess and can also refer to a celebrated female singer, a woman of outstanding talent in the world of opera,

Divo. Yes, there is a male equivalent to the familiar opera diva. It's usually a tenor.

Beautiful, dramatic, soaring singing is only one task of an opera diva or divo. They also must put some oomph to their voice since the big major opera productions are in large halls. The persons sitting in the last seat in the last row must hear the song.

That's not all. It helps to be a good actor or actress too.

An opera remember is a drama. This suggests more than just being able to sing a part. You've got to act it too.

There is one more chore for the opera singer. They must know their songs and parts from memory. They must sing and speak it in the language it is written in. That may be Italian, German, French, Russian, or English.

The standard three opera voices for the females are the **alto, soprano,** and **mezzo-soprano.** The highest range is the soprano. The lowest is the mezzo-soprano. There's also the **coloratura.** She is a soprano but a specialized soprano who can add a light embellishment to her singing. The standard three opera voices for the men are the **tenor, baritone,** and **bass.** The tenor hits the highest notes. The bass hits the deep resonate, low notes, and the baritone falls somewhere in between the tenor and bass.

Since it's a musical drama, everyone has a designated role. Almost always, the leading lady singer is the heroine. This part usually falls to the soprano. If the hero is a man, it's usually the tenor. If the character is a man of majesty and stature or is a despicable villain, this requires a big, barreling voice. That's usually the bass.

* * * * *

Opera composers range far and wide over many subject areas to find the right story to set to music. I'll spotlight one written by someone other than the three recognized giants of opera, Verdi, Wagner, and Mozart.

German composer Carl Maria von Weber (1726-1826) got the brainstorm for his opera *Der Freischütz* (The Free Shooter) (1821) from the same place that countless other opera composers got theirs. That is from a legend, tale, or an old story. The story was an ancient German folk song and legend for von Weber.

He crammed his production with ghosts, magic bullets, and hellhounds. His main character did much bargaining with the devil. He had a spectacular, big, catchy overture to get the audience going. It's a good thing he did because, unlike Mozart and Verdi's operas, it did not stand the test of time as a staple in the opera hall.

I chose von Weber's opera not because of its enduring popularity or lack thereof. But to show that opera composers don't merely pull their stories from thin air. There is some basis in fact or fantasy, and often a combination of both, in the choice of material for their opera.

* * * * *

Opera like the symphony and the concerto changed over time. It had its distinct periods of growth, expansion, and change. In the 12th century, there was Medieval Opera. It primarily drew heavily, if not exclusively, on religious, churchly, and heavenly stories. It is referred to as liturgical drama.

Next was the baroque opera. It had a run from roughly 1600 to 1750. In the early years of this period, the opera mainly was the spoken word **recitative** with very little singing. That soon changed. The one who changed it was an Italian Claudio Monteverdi (1567–1643). His opera *L'Orfeo* (1607) was a sort of mixed media production. It combined poetry, music, scenery, and acting together. Nearly four centuries later, opera still uses the template that Monteverdi established. One more thing about this period of opera.

Starting with Monteverdi's opera and others in the 1600s, opera was not the preserve of the royalty and super-rich patrons. There were designated **seasons** in which the public bought tickets and attended operas. Still, for the most part, during that time, opera didn't free itself from the preserve of the upper classes.

It was regarded as highbrow fare for the amusement and enjoyment of the wealthy and nobility.

The next small advance came with the classical opera in the late 1700s. This was the heyday of Mozart with his operas. There was dark drama, *Don Giovanni* (1787), and the magic and fantasy of *The Magic Flute*.

Wagner (1813-1883) and Verdi made the giant leap in opera in the mid-19th century. Wagner didn't like the word opera. This was just too commonplace for him. He branded his works" dramas with music words." His point was that the singing was necessary, but he was writing epic stuff. He wanted audiences to focus on that and not have a soprano or bass detract from that.

He made sure that audiences understood the written word, not just the singing that made his operas. He wrote his opera stories. The story writing in opera is called the **libretto.** Before Wagner took personal charge of the writing, it was customary for opera composers to leave the actual writing of the storyline to someone else," a librettist."

Wagner leaned heavily on German folklore and myths. He used leitmotifs to highlight specific characters in his biggest ticket operas, *The Flying Dutchman* (1844), *Lohengrin* (1848), and *Tannhauser* (1845)

However, Wagner's piece de resistance is the all-time ponderous, top-heavy, drawn-out *Ring Cycle*. It takes three to four days of sitting, watching, and listening to get through the work. It is a thunder of sound and movement of myth, fable, philosophy, and German nationalism, all rolled into one operatic ball. This wasn't a one-year wonder in writing. Try 26 years (1848-1876). Whew!!!

Leitmotif is a short but distinctive piece of music that is supposed to conjure up an idea or a character in an opera.

74 A Young Person's Guide to Classical Music

🎧 Recommended Listening

Richard Wagner, *Götterdämmerung: Twilight of the Gods*
London Philharmonic Orchestra
www.youtube.com/watch?v=wXh5JprKqiU

✷ ✷ ✷ ✷ ✷

Wagner's works have dominated operatic stages since the late 1800s. There is a vast body of music literature and analysis (not always complimentary). His life reads like a what's what of adventure, controversy, and tragedy. He was a scoundrel, philanderer, political rebel, fugitive, and notorious antisemite. Adolph Hitler's deification of him and his music has been recounted countless times. Yet, he still stands as the primary game-changer for opera from the mid-1800s on.

Verdi viewed opera a lot differently than Wagner. He loved good singing. The bel canto singer was front and center in his works. He wrote lots of them—25. His best-known are the beloved staples of every global opera house, *Othello, Macbeth, Falstaff, Rigoletto, Ii Travatoree, La Traviata,* written between 1839 and 1893.

Verdi wasn't content to leave opera to the crooners. He stretched, fleshed out, and experimented with style, harmony, and orchestration. This gave his works and opera then and now such a distinctive character. Verdi, as Wagner did one more feat with the opera.

He took it out of the sole province of the kings, queens, emperors, empresses, the wealthy royal patronage, and the upper class. He turned it into an art form for regular people. Verdi did it by writing some of his operas about the lives of ordinary folk, people who were shunned, trodden on, looked down on by the upper classes. He wanted opera to tell the raw but realistic story of the tragedies and triumphs of ordinary people. This gritty realism style in opera is called the **verismo.** The new trend was to tell a story in opera that mirrored real life. The characters in the stories were usually from the lower classes.

Verismo is Italian for '"realism,"' from *vero,* meaning "true."

For instance, Verdi's *La Traviata* (1852) isn't about the quirks of the rich, famous, and nobility. It's a story of a courtesan (prostitute in less polite language). Her saga is a saga of the tragedies of ordinary people who lead everyday lives in ordinary society. Like so many true-to-life operas, Hollywood couldn't resist pilfering the storyline from *La Traviata*. In *Pretty Woman* (1990), Julia Roberts plays a high-class call girl who Richard Gere, a wealthy mogul, pants after with all the ups and downs and agony that that kind of would-be relationship brings with it. Hollywood being Hollywood, it had to have a happy ending. La Traviata didn't.

French composer George Bizet went one better. He filled his ground-breaking *Carmen* (1875) with earthy, in-your-face, gritty real-life realism. He fills the drama with a motley cast of vagabonds, thieves, prostitutes, and other social outcasts. It tells the story of more ill-gotten love, desire, tortured emotional conflict, lust, and ultimately heartbreak. There's no surprise that it ends in tragedy.

Giacomo Puccini (1858-1924), like Verdi and Bizet, was also onto something significant with his three big-ticket operas, *Tosca* (1900), *Il tabarro* (1918), and especially his smash it, *Madama Butterfly* (1898), which is about lost love. They are verismo operas in the truest sense. They're based on the events in the lives of everyday people, not myths, fantasy, and folklore. Neither does he cater in his storylines to the foibles of the rich and the nobility.

> *"And she entered, fragrant as a flower, and fell into my arms.*
> *Oh, sweet kisses, lingering caresses.*
> *Slowly, trembling, I gazed upon her beauty.*

*Now my dream of true love is lost forever.
My last hour has flown, and I die, hopeless, and never have I loved life more."*

—*Tosca*

Recommended Listening

Giacomo Puccini, *"Un bel di vedremo"*
from *Madama Butterfly*, Act 2
Maria Callas, Orchestra del Teatro alla Scala
www.youtube.com/watch?v=sLcbfF9ypmM

* * * * *

Opera took another turn following the era of Verdi and Wagner that impacted American musical productions in the 1930s. American musicals during those years began to look and sound like operas. They attained a popularity that had been the sole reserve of Italian and German opera before then. George Gershwin's *Porgy and Bess* (1935) was an opera heavily influenced by jazz styles.

Leonard Bernstein's *Candide* (1956), with its sweeping, lyrical passages and farcical parodies of opera, was like *Porgy*, a big Broadway production. However, it is regarded as part of the opera repertory. Popular later musicals such as *Show Boat, West Side Story, Brigadoon, Sweeney Todd: The Demon Barber of Fleet Street, Passion, Evita, The Light in the Piazza, The Phantom of the Opera,* and others tell dramatic stories through complex music and the tradition of opera.

The operatic reach didn't end there. There are rock-influenced musicals, such as *Tommy* (1969) and *Jesus Christ Superstar* (1971), *Les Misérables* (1980), *Rent* (1996), *Spring Awakening* (2006), and *Natasha, Pierre & The Great Comet of 1812* (2012), employ various operatic conventions, such as through composition, recitative instead of dialogue, and leitmotifs.

Some opera composers discovered a hard and bitter fact of musical life about their operas. All were not destined to be an all-time favorite, audience pleasers as Verdi, Mozart, and Wagner's operas. Many operas died a quick death. In some cases, though, their overtures survived and became major stand-alone famous works played regularly on concert bills.

I mentioned von Weber's overture as one example. In other instances, even operas that become major and enduring audience favorites, their overtures also became significant works. Mozart, Verdi, and Wagner's overtures fit that bill. Their names are virtual musical household names. Here are five of their operatic overtures that are standard pieces on concert bills:

The Magic Flute
(Die Zauberflöte), K. 620
Wolfgang Amadeus Mozart, 1791

Tannhäuser, WWV 70
Richard Wagner, 1845

The Marriage of Figaro
(Le nozze di Figaro), K. 492
Wolfgang Amadeus Mozart, 1786

The Barber of Seville
(Il barbiere di Siviglia)
Gioachino Rossini, 1816

William Tell
(Guglielmo Tell)
Gioachino Rossini, 1829

* * * * *

Perhaps the most outstanding innovation has been in presenting opera as a classical music art for the masses. The first live televised broadcasts of opera were in 1951. The New York Metropolitan Opera (the Met) broadcasts practically became weekly household radio features. The next step up for opera broadcasting was the movie houses. In 2007, Met performances were shown in over 424 theaters in 350 U. S. cities. Verdi's. *La bohème* went out to 671 screens worldwide.

European opera houses and festivals, including the Royal Opera in London, La Scala in Milan, the Salzburg Festival, La Fenice in Venice, and the Maggio Musicale in Florence, also transmit their productions to theaters in cities around the world. That includes 90 cities in the U. S.

First radio, then television, then the movie theaters, now there's the internet. Enterprising opera companies in Europe and the U. S. offer an online digital video download of their productions.

* * * * *

I started this discussion of opera with a quote from Wagner, opera's other greatc master, Verdi. It's only fitting then to end this discussion with a quote from Wagner's other great operatic master.

"The error in the art-genre of Opera consists herein: a Means of expression (Music) has been made the end, while the End of expression (the Drama) has been made a means."

Wagner punched all the buttons in this short quip about opera—art, genre, music, a means of expression, drama, and music. That's hardly an error in opera. These elements of opera have made it an everlasting object of pleasure, controversy, and fascination through four-plus centuries.

Opera past and present ranks as one of the big three of classical music alongside the symphony and the concerto. Classical music, though, is not all bigness and grandeur. Let's drop things down a bit and look at the big three's musical smaller cousins.

5

The Smaller Works

"It was "patched together from pieces
filched here and there."
—Ludwig van Beethoven

Beethoven had just finished his *String Quartet in C-sharp Minor* in the summer of 1826. He described it as a kind of patchwork work, like a junkyard sculpture, tossed together from pieces here and there. At least that's the impression he gave his publisher in a note to him. Yet, he was not happy.

Beethoven almost certainly showed his wry sense of humor in depicting his string quartet as a scrap heap work. It had to be a joke. His string quartet is a masterpiece and a regular on concert bills. However, Beethoven put his finger on something about one of his small works. It is small. I'll get to the significance of that shortly only because, as its name-quartet- suggests, it has four instruments. I want to work up to that by progressing through works based on the number of instruments and musicians involved in a particular work.

First, there's the **sonata.** Yes, I know the name so struck Hyundai that it branded one of its models "sonata." But we're talking music. You can't get any more basic than a sonata. It is a work for a single instrument. The instrument might be a piano, violin, oboe, cello, trumpet, or clarinet. Sonata comes from Italian. It means to "sound."

The notes are arranged following the form developed with symphonies and concertos in the nineteenth century that I discussed earlier. There's a fast movement, a slow movement, and a rapid ending movement. This is not set in stone. There might be only one or two movements in the sonata. It may start slow and even end slow. So, there's flexibility with it.

It is a form that has a lot of adaptability. It can be a stand-alone work. The greatest classical composers wrote many great sonatas. They have stood the test of time in playing and popularity. One of them is often ranked as one of the best of the best. It has a name recognizable to millions within and without the classical music world. That's Beethoven's *Piano Sonata No. 14 in C-Sharp Minor* (1801). Almost no one outside the classical move world knows its formal listing name. They do know it as the *Moonlight Sonata.*

This is yet another of the many classical music works that usually the composer's enterprising publisher attaches a catchy name. A sidenote Beethoven did not name it the *Moonlight Sonata.* It was done strictly to give it widespread name recognition, to promote better and market it, and of course, make more money from it. Think about trying to sell and get the public to remember *Sonata No. 14* or "Moonlight"? You get the idea.

Indeed, one of the accomplishments the late Los Angeles Laker basketball superstar Kobe Bryant said he wanted to do off the court was to play Beethoven's *Moonlight Sonata*. Mission accomplished!

Recommended Listening

Ludwig van Beethoven, *Piano Sonata No. 14 in C-Sharp Minor, "Moonlight Sonata"* (1801)
Kobe Bryant, Piano
www.youtube.com/watch?v=jct6xeTmf9k

The *Moonlight Sonata* is one of 32 piano sonatas Beethoven wrote. Take special note of the numbering, "No.

14" When you see a number in a composer's work, here's what it means.

Numbers. They identify a specific work and indicate the work's sequence. *No. 14,* then, was the 14th sonata Beethoven wrote.

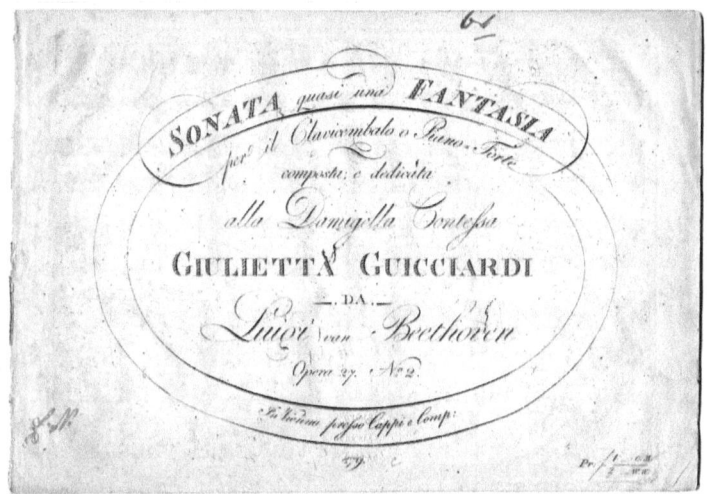

* * * * *

The sonata is one of the two standard forms of organizing, interpreting, and analyzing concert music. More specifically, it's one of a symphony or concerto movements. The other is the **fugue.**

Fugue. Imagine two or more voices singing, facing each other, and singing at each other. They have one subject or theme of their song. The song is repeated at different pitches or what's called imitation. That is just repetition at different pitches. This repeatedly recurs during the work. Thus, we have the fugue. In musical jargon, it's called counterpoint.

The general idea of the sonata structure is that it's supposed to have some center tone within the arrangement of pitches and/or chords in a musical work. Think of it as a hierarchy of notes.

The *Grove Concise Dictionary of Music* puts it this way: "The main form of the group embodying the 'sonata principle,' the most important principle of musical structure from the Classical period to the 20th century: that material first stated in a complementary key be restated in the home key."

During the Baroque period, it was common for musicians to write a sonata as dance music. Picture this, a village dance scene in that day, with a musician plucking away on a lute while the villagers make merry. The sonata is not just for dance or a solo instrument. Not to be confused with the sonata, the sonata form is the *structure of an individual movement* in a **sonata**, a **symphony**, or a **concerto**.

* * * * *

We come back to the orchestra. Composers, as noted, wrote three, then later, four-movement works. During this period, they got bigger and expanded the number of instruments. Here's a quick recap of those movements again with their names.

- Slow movement, an a**ndante,** an a**dagio,** or a **largo.**
- Dance movement, frequently **minuet and trio** or—especially later in the classical period—a s**cherzo and trio.**
- Finale in a faster tempo, often in a **sonata-rondo** form.

Notice in the movements there is the notation "sonata form."

Composers wrote the one instrument sonata because they were easy to write, easy to score, and easy to play. They also had something else in mind. They were musical vehicles to showcase the composer's musical prowess on their specialty instrument. Beethoven was a master pianist. So, it's not hard to figure out why he'd write so many sonatas, many of them for the piano. There was more than a little financial interest in writing a sonata. It could lead to more paid jobs, either providing music at the royal court or for the composer/musician playing at the private soirees of the rich.

Recommended Listening

Johann Sebastian Bach, *Violin Sonata No. 1*, BWV 1001
Itzhak Perlman, Violin
www.youtube.com/watch?v=etB8MAjNaz0

Alberto Ginastera, *Piano Sonata No. 1*, Op. 22
Horacio Lavandera, Piano
www.youtube.com/watch?v=7-lcnVAoLRE

From the Concert Seat

George Bridgetower was a prodigious musical talent of Afro-Caribbean ancestry who gave successful violin concerts in Paris, London, Bath, and Bristol in 1789. He performed in around 50 concerts in London theatres between 1789 and 1799. In the spring of 1789, Bridgetower performed to great acclaim at the Abbaye de Panthemont in Paris, with Thomas Jefferson and his family in attendance. The one composer, though, who would have burned Bridgetower's name in the classical music world's books for eternity was Beethoven. That is if things hadn't gone badly awry.

On a visit to Vienna in 1803, he performed with Beethoven. The master was impressed. So impressed that he dedicated his *Violin Sonata No. 9 in A Major* to Bridgetower. Though no offense was intended, he even plopped on the humorous title.

Sonata per un mulattico lunatico. Beethoven was so eager to display it that he gave a public performance at the Augarten Theatre on May 24, 1803, before the ink was barely dry on it. Bridgetower played the violin part so well that Beethoven leaped up and exclaimed, "Noch einmal, mein lieber Bursch!" ("Once more, my dear fellow!"). The master wasn't finished. He was so grateful that he forked over his tuning fork to Bridgetower. It's on display today in the British Library.

Alas, the happy story didn't have a happy ending. Both "Bs" were top-rate virtuoso performers. And both had strong temperaments and egos. They fell out over Bridgetower's purported insult to a female friend of Beethoven's. In a pique, what would have been known for posterity as the Bridgetower Sonata instead Beethoven renamed the Kreutzer Sonata after Beethoven's other violin playing pal violin virtuoso Rudolphe Kreutzer. There's a final sad note. Kreutzer said the work was too complicated and never played it. No matter, his name is the name that the world knows the sonata as today.

✻ ✻ ✻ ✻ ✻

The Trio

If three persons are singing together in pop music or R & B music, it's a trio. The Kingston Trio, for example, is well known in the pop world. It's the same in classical music. The major difference is the trio is not singers but instrumentalists. More instruments were developed and came on board for use. They needed more players to play them at one time. It soon became a numbers game.

The trio could also be for three separate musical parts. The trio can consist of varied instruments. However, the almost standard trio instruments are violin, bass, and the piano. Trios are heavily weighted toward string instruments and are typically in the form of three movements: fast-slow-fast.

The types of trios are infinite. There are flute trios, violin trios, viola trios, piano trios, cello trios, organ trios, and so forth. A trio can also be inserted into just about any more considerable work. Bach inserts a trio in his famed *Brandenburg Concerto No. 1* (1721). Two oboes and bassoon play together. Then he has a third part where three oboes play together in unison.

Here is a more complete list of the varied trio instrument combinations that can make up a trio.

- Brass trio (horn, trumpet, trombone)
- Clarinet-cello-piano trio (clarinet, cello, piano)
- Clarinet-viola-piano trio (clarinet, viola, piano)
- Clarinet-violin-piano trio (clarinet, violin, piano)
- Flute, viola, and harp (flute, viola, harp)
- Harmonica trio (chromatic harmonica, bass harmonica, chord harmonica)
- Horn trio (valved or natural horn, violin, and piano)
- Jazz trio (piano or guitar, acoustic bass or bass guitar, drum kit)

- Organ trio (Hammond organ, drummer, jazz guitarist or saxophone)
- Power trio (electric guitar, bass guitar, drum kit)

 **Recommended Listening**

Franz Schubert, *Piano Trio No. 1 in B flat*
Klavier Trio
www.youtube.com/watch?v=y6HTkmXtoqY

* * * * *

The Quartet

Add another instrument to the trio, and now you have a Quartet. It's a group of four instruments: most commonly violins, a viola, and a cello. These are the string instruments. This type of quartet is the string quartet. The form usually follows its big brother, the symphony, a fast, slow, and a speedball ending. There are usually, but not always, four movements. Sometimes there is a **minuet** included. That was especially the case during the Baroque period.

The minuet can be slow, stately, and in dance form. That's because that was the rage of the European nobility in the 17th, 18th, and 19th Centuries. They danced into the night to the minuet at court balls. Their love of the stately dance wasn't lost on composers. They thought, why not instead of just listening to a piece, let's make it so that some of it anyway can be danced to as well.

Composers didn't stop with three or four instrument works. Since the violin, cello, and viola aren't the only things going on in the orchestra, they soon wrote **quintets** (five instruments), **sextets** (six instruments), **septets** (seven instruments), and **octets** (eight instruments). Some composers wrote for many players. They kept the same fast-slow-fast and/or minuet form.

 **Recommended Listening**

Chevalier de Saint-George, *Quartet No. 3 in F Minor,* Op. 14
Apollon Quartet
www.youtube.com/watch?v=rOYJu_IWqhU

Franz Schubert, *Piano Quintet in A Major, "Trout"*
Berliner Philharmoniker Soloists
www.youtube.com/watch?v=vWDHtlqgwMY

Peter Ilich Tchaikovsky, String Sextet in D Minor, *"Souvenir de Florence"*
Tchaikovsky String Sextet
www.youtube.com/watch?v=Q6X2XcqjqMw

Felix Mendelssohn, *Octet in E-flat Major,* Op. 20
International Chamber Music Festival
www.youtube.com/watch?v=Vw1kcQ-QbZw

The Smaller Works

A string quartet in performance.
From left to right, violin 1, violin 2, cello, viola

Nearly all the best-known composers churned out one or more quartets at one time or another. They liked that form. It had the requisite melody, tempo, and pitch changes common to symphonies. Composers could pack a lot of musical ideas into a smaller work. This gives you an idea of how popular the quartet was with the major composers of their day.

- Franz Joseph Haydn (68)
- Wolfgang Amadeus Mozart (23)
- Ludwig van Beethoven (16)
- Franz Schubert (15)
- Felix Mendelssohn (6)
- Johannes Brahms (3)
- Antonín Dvorak (14)

* * * * *

You can see from the prodigious numbers that the undisputed master of the quartet was Haydn. He loved them and wrote so many of them in part because they allowed him to work out musical ideas in a relatively short musical space. And in equal part, because he worked for a royal house. The quartets were pleasant and entertaining music suited for royal gatherings.

Haydn was so enamored of the quartet that he felt he had to publicly apologize when he could not complete his D Minor string quartet in 1803. It wasn't because he had run out of ideas or passion for the quartet. It was because of age. He was 71 (he lived six more years).

Haydn felt his physical powers slipping. He put his apology for not finishing the work on the score (the written musical sheet), "Gone is all my strength, old and weak am I." Unfinished or not, Haydn still displayed the vibrancy and power of a small work in this quartet. As one reviewer aptly put it, it "is gentle, pensive, simple rhythmically and formally." It typified then how a smaller work, be it the sonata, trio, or quartet, could deliver the complete musical goods in a small package, and most importantly, with a small number of instruments.

Interestingly, in all the vast literature on classical music, there are loads of juicy, memorable quotes from the greats about their music, art, politics, beliefs, and philosophy of life. They wax expansively on just about any and everything. However, with one or two exceptions, they have little to say about the most essential tools of their craft: the instruments. That's a pity since just about every one of classical music's instruments has an exciting history of how it found its way into the composer's hands.

Now it's on to the instruments.

6

The Instruments

*"It's easy to play any musical instrument:
all you have to do is touch the right key at the right time,
and the instrument will play itself. "*
—*Johann Sebastian Bach*

I get what Bach is saying here. If you know what you are doing when you pick up an instrument, then everything will fall into place. Of course, that's easy for Bach to say. In classical music, he was one of the most fantastic organ virtuoso performers of his day, or maybe any day. He was undoubtedly correct that we'd be stuck with the voice alone as the instrument of record without the instruments. That wouldn't make a concerto, symphony, sonata, trio, or quartet. For that, you need the instruments.

Let's start with the string instruments. The violin is far and away the oldest and best known of the string instruments. It has four strings. It is small and played with a bow. The strings are made of horsehair or steel, or nylon. The sound comes from the plucking of are drawing the bow across the strings. They vibrate. What you hear are those vibrations. It's a bit more complicated than that. The strings are not all the same.

They have different **frequencies.** What's that? It's how many times something occurs (vibrates) in one second. The strings can be adjusted. They have to be adjusted to change frequencies. They could be high, low, or any point in between. It's tuned to a particular key. The parts of the violin are named after parts of the body. The front is called the "belly." The back is called the "back." The sides are the "ribs. "The strings go from near the top of the "neck" down the "fingerboard" and on to the "tailpiece." The strings go across the bridge halfway between the end of the fingerboard and the tailpiece.

* * * * *

The **violin** is considered the most essential instrument in any orchestra. It's so vital that it makes up nearly half the instruments in an orchestra. There are so many of them that the orchestras divide them and seat the players in two sections. One section is the "first violins." The other is the "second violins." Because the violin is one of the oldest and best-known instruments, composers have long taken to it as the instrument to write something grand. Mozart, Beethoven, Haydn, and many other classical composers wrote violin concertos that showcased the violin.

Recommended Listening

Ludwig van Beethoven, *Violin Concerto in D Major*
Itzhak Perlman, Violin
Berliner Philharmoniker
www.youtube.com/watch?v=cokCgWPRZPg

From the Concert Seat

The instruments in a symphony do not just blare away. They stand for something. The something is the composer's musical ideas. They express those ideas. Gustav Mahler was very explicit about that in his four-movement *Symphony No. 1, "The Titan."* Let's take a snippet from the third movement of the symphony. A principal idea behind it is a hunter's funeral and a procession of animals that follows. He presents it first with solo double bass. A bassoon and tuba follow this. Then the whole orchestra picks up the theme played over the top of the canon in the oboe. If you know this and close your eyes and open your imagination, you can see the animals parade by.

The violin has a close cousin—the **viola.** It's a bit larger. It has four strings, and it is also played with a bow. It has a deeper sound. The **cello** is another part of the string instrument family. It's larger still. It has an even deeper sound. The cello also has four strings. This sound is called the bass sound.

👂 Recommended Listening

Franz Joseph Haydn, *Cello Concerto No. 1 in C Major*
Concertgebouw Chamber Orchestra
www.youtube.com/watch?v=4Mb4HbxKNzs

The other string family member is the **double bass.** It has the lowest, or most resonant sound, of all the string instruments.

There are a couple of other differences within the string instruments. The cello and the double bass are upright instruments. The musician sits or even stands while playing the cello and bass. The violin and viola are horizontal instruments. They are played with the broad part underneath the violinist or violist's chin. The other prominent member of the string family is the guitar. It is plucked.

A not-so-principal member of the family is the harp. It is the biggest of all the string instruments. It is very upright. It's also a plucked instrument.

I've mentioned plucking a couple of times. As you've

already discovered, classical music has a term, lots of terms, for everything in the music. Plucking has its term. In classical music jargon, it's not called plucking. That's too commonplace sounding. It's called the **pizzicato.** It's a thrilling moment in a violin concerto to hear and see the violist plucking the string with their hand rather than drawing the bow across them.

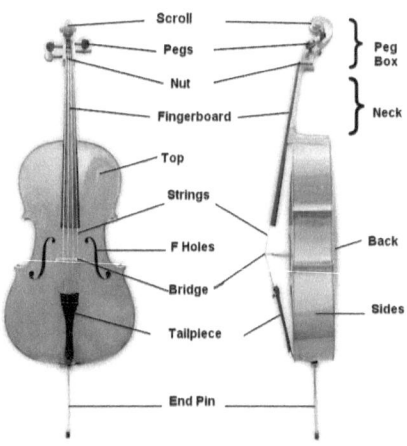

Parts of a cello

* * * * *

Woodwinds

In days gone by, the woodwinds were made of wood. That's how they got their name, the woodwinds. Today, many of them are made of metal or plastic. I'll name the five that are standard instruments in any symphony orchestra for our purposes.

I didn't list the saxophone because it is not standard fare in the orchestra. They are the **flute** and its kin, the **piccolo,** the **clarinet,** the **bassoon,** and the **oboe.** But believe it or not, the sax is a woodwind, not a brass instrument, though many mistakenly think it is. It's considered a woodwind because it's played like the clarinet. The bassoon can be a heavy load weight-wise. Many players have either a neck strap or a seat strap to lighten the load.

You play the flute, sax, clarinet, and piccolo by blowing across, into, or through the top of the mouthpiece.

* * * * *

Brass

The **trumpet** is the brass instrument that most are familiar with. It is an instrument that the ancients used to mark a call to arms—a triumph in battles, festivities, parades, and processions. It's been around longer than any other instruments, 3000 years to be exact.

The brasses are blown in the same way by blowing against a cup-shaped mouthpiece. This is how the pitch is changed to make differing sounds.

The **trombone** is the oddest played instrument. It is played by pushing and pulling back and forth on its slide to change the sound and the length of the tube. It has a deeper sound than the trumpet and can play a wide range of notes. Another interesting thing about the trombone is that there are many different types. The **tenor trombone, contrabass trombone, bass trombone, alto trombone,**

soprano trombone, and **piccolo trombone** each produce a different sound. The difference is called a **range,** or range of sound.

Besides being the heftiest, the brass instrument that looks the oddest of all is the **tuba.** It is a relative newcomer to orchestras. It is played by depressing the valves. It has the lowest sound of all the instruments in an orchestra. There are three to six of them.

Recommended Listening

Franz Joseph Haydn, *Trumpet Concerto in E Flat Major*
Tine Thing Helseth, Trumpet
Norwegian Symphony Orchestra
www.youtube.com/watch?v=rO2L9Q06CTE

Wolfgang Amadeus Mozart, *Clarinet Concerto in A Major*
Arngunnur Árnadóttir, Clarinet
Iceland Symphony Orchestra
www.youtube.com/watch?v=YT_63UntRJE

* * * * *

The Percussions

The **drum** is the percussion instrument that instantly comes to mind. Whether you are from 2 to 92 years old, it's the easiest to play. All you have to do is take a stick or your hand and beat it. Now let's put some names to the drum.

The timpani is the two kettle-shaped drums that sit at the back of the orchestra, with the drummer usually seated. There's the **snare drum** and the **bass drum.**

Other instruments in the percussion section are usually positioned close to the drums. They are the cymbals, triangles, and tambourine(s). They are played by shaking, tapping, or beating them. They are there to provide extra rhythm to a particular piece.

* * * * *

The Keyboards

Most people stop and start with the **piano.** That's reasonable. The piano is the instrument that many young persons can remember getting their first and, in most cases, their last musical lesson on. In addition to being along with the violin, the best-known instrument, it does double duty. It is both a keyboard and a string instrument.

How do we get the sound? It has a keyboard consisting of a row of 88 black and white keys (small levers). The keys play the different notes or **pitches** (levels of sound). The pianist presses down on or strikes the keys with one or both hands while seated. This causes the hammer (joined to the string) to strike the strings. Striking the keys hard produces greater hammer force hitting the strings. The greater the force, the greater or louder the sound.

The sound is the vibration of the strings. It's the same as mentioned earlier with the violin. The notes are sustained, even when the keys are released by the fingers and thumbs, using pedals at the instrument's base. The first **fortepianos** in the 1700s had a quieter sound and smaller dynamic range.

When you say piano, generally, it stops there. After all, a piano is a piano. There are two major types. One is the **grand piano.** It's bigger and has a fuller body sound.

The other is the more miniature **upright piano.** It is the one most frequently used in concert performances. That's mainly because it takes up less space on the stage. There are other piano types. There are **studio, console, toy, mini, prepared, structured, pedal, microtone,** and **transposing** pianos. In the 21st Century, there are electric and digital pianos.

The piano is universally popular for another reason. It's a marvelously versatile instrument. It has a wide pitch range, can play loud two or more chords, louder and softer notes, and more than one melodic line simultaneously.

The piano has undergone many changes in 300 years since it was first invented. It started as a **harpsichord** and then progressed to the **clavichord** to the **fortepiano.** The problem with these early forerunners of the modern-day piano is that you couldn't vary the sound (pitches). Everything sounded the same. Adding more keys to the instrument extended the range of sound from low bass to a high pitch range.

The Instruments

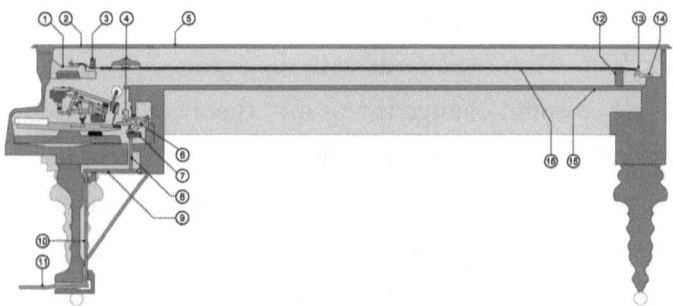

Parts of a Piano. ① frame ② lid, front part ③ capo bar ④ damper ⑤ lid, back part ⑥ damper mechanism ⑦ sostenuto rail ⑧ pedal mechanism, rods ⑨ ⑩ ⑪ pedals: right (sustain/damper), middle (sostenuto), left (soft/una-corda) ⑫ bridge ⑬ hitch pin ⑭ frame ⑮ sound board ⑯ string

 **Recommended Listening**

Edvard Grieg, *Piano Concerto in A Minor,* Op. 16
Arthur Rubenstein, Piano
London Symphony Orchestra
www.youtube.com/watch?v=I1Yoyz6_Los

* * * * *

I mentioned that the piano is universally loved and played because of its versatility. The piano can be used for solo, melodic, or accompanying instruments in any musical setting, from large-scale symphonies to accompaniment for a vocalist. Mozart, Haydn, Beethoven, and Bach were phenomenal keyboard wizards. They found that they could use the keyboard to experiment with all sorts of melodic and harmonic chords with the piano.

They could change them, mix them up, or just interplay with them simultaneously. It's an instrument to learn new pieces and songs to lead in performance. I have seen more conductors that play the piano than any other instrument. They can play parts of the symphony they are conducting on the piano. This helps them work out their interpretation of a symphonic work they are conducting. Pianos are the most widely used instrument to teach music theory, music history, and music appreciation classes.

The instruments that are standard fare in orchestras today—the woodwinds, the strings, the percussion, and the brass sections didn't just happen. Each has its unique history. There's a story behind how they eventually made their way into the orchestra.

The other part of their story is how they make the music. In 1844 French composer Hector Berlioz thought long and hard about the instruments and their place in classical music. So hard that he wrote an entire treatise on instrumentation. *Traité d'instrumentation et d'orchestration modernes (Treatise on Instrumentation and Orchestration).*

Berlioz did more than just write about it or compose works that used a few principal instruments. He went big, very big. In his transformative *Symphonie fantastique* (1830), Berlioz reached, maybe overreached, for any and every one of the instruments available in colossal numbers. He used the instruments to depict the events in his symphony. The symphony told of the agonies of lost love, his lost love. He aimed to use instruments to help tell the story of that agony and all the events surrounding it.

Here's an example from the fourth movement, "March to the Scaffold."

He uses heavy low bass instruments to affect the military beat. Blaring horns continue and enhance the marching beat. A solo clarinet with a haunting tune represents the last conscious thought of the soon-to-be-executed man. Finally, a snare drum completes the gruesome musical scene by representing the fall of the guillotine—complete with a **crescendo.**

Crescendo. This is a gradual increase in the volume or intensity of sound in a musical passage until it reaches a big bang of sound.

Berlioz went even bigger seven years later in his *Grande Messe des morts (Requiem)*, 1837. He used four flutes, two oboes, two English horns, four clarinets, 12 horns, eight bassoons, 25 first violins, 25-second violins, 20 violas, 20 violoncellos, 18 double basses, eight pairs of timpani, four tam-tams (a type of gong), bass drum, and 10 pairs of cymbals; four brass choirs placed in various parts of the hall, each consisting of four trumpets, four trombones, two tubas, and four ophicleides (a large, now obsolete brass instrument); and a chorus of 80 sopranos, 80 altos, 60 tenors, and 70 basses.

How the orchestra managed to get all those instruments on one stage has to be one of the feats of the ages. I end my discussion of Berlioz's instruments and his instrumental extravagance to show that the instruments are the real show in classical music.

7

The Soloist

> "He devoted himself to the concerto until the
> accompaniment, which is rather complicated,
> had been practiced to perfection."
> —Sergei Rachmaninoff

Russian composer and pianist Sergei Rachmaninoff (1873-1943) is describing the demanding rehearsal he had preparing for the premiere of his phenomenally challenging *Piano Concerto No. 3 in D Minor* in New York in 1909. It had to be correct. Rachmaninoff was delighted that the concerto was practiced and rehearsed to perfection. He was scheduled to be the piano soloist for his work. He, not the orchestra, would be center stage.

There's almost nothing like the soloist in classical music. The soloist is the one performer who stands or sits in front of an orchestra playing the solo part in a Mozart, Beethoven, Bach, Brahms, Haydn, or Tchaikovsky piano or violin concerto. All eyes and attention are riveted on them. The soloist knows it. They must be at the top of their musical game when they get their cue to hit the first key of the piano or bow the first violin string.

If they please the audience, they can be assured that some, many, or all in the audience will instantly spring to their feet with shouts of "bravo" and "encore." In most cases, after taking their many requisite bows, they will oblige and play one of the probably many pieces they have ready-made to go for just such an eventuality in their repertoire.

Solo is Italian, meaning alone. It is a piece or section of music played or sung by a single performer, the soloist.

Recommended Listening

Camille Saint-Saens, *Piano Concerto No. 5 in F Major "Egyptian"*
Shai Sluzki, Piano
Buchmann-Mehta School of Music Symphony Orchestra
www.youtube.com/watch?v=Yki1z2NfO-o

The Soloist

* * * * *

Bach, Handel, Mozart, and Beethoven are the unrivaled giants of instrumental classical music. Several other names deserve to sit on the top shelf with them. My first introduction to one of them was the tune I heard many times, a melody that has danced into the ears of tens of thousands of brides, grooms, and wedding guests. That tune is the well-known "Wedding March" from *A Midsummer Night's Dream in E Major* (1826), written by 17-year-old Felix Mendelssohn (Germany, 1809-47), and he was off to the races with his career after he penned it. Mendelssohn was a master at taking musical ideas from contemporaries and turning them into his masterpieces of sound.

His five symphonies, two piano concertos, and violin concerto feature gorgeous color, lots of expression, warmth, sublime beauty, power, flowing melodies, and even unpredictable rhythms. They set a high standard for composers, even those of his own time. When it came to style, he was a real throwback to Mozart. I mention him first in this chapter because he was a brilliant piano soloist.

He and the other master soloists of that era extended the range of individual works and shoved the solo performer to center stage. They mostly wrote for and played the piano, but their skill and virtuosity extended to the cello, violin, and oboe. These were the instruments they wowed and dazzled audiences with, particularly the nobility. They often performed in exclusive recitals for the crowned heads of Europe, thus ensuring big paydays and much royal patronage and favoritism.

Mendelssohn brought the same sunburst beauty and power to his piano works. His *Seven Character Pieces and Songs Without Words* (1829-45), for instance, prove that true virtuosity can often be found simply in the playing of a piece.

> **From My Concert Seat**
>
> **I've often noted that pianists will sometimes close their eyes and talk to the keys while lovingly caressing them. I watched noted Russian pianist Olga Korn do this while playing the elegant second movement of Edvard Grieg's *Piano Concerto in A Minor* (1858) at a concert of the New Mexico Philharmonic. It was a pure, sensual connection between an artist and her instrument, and there was something beautiful about it that came through in the music.**

Franz Schubert (Germany, 1797-1828), like Mendelssohn, didn't live long. He died at age 31. As short as his life was, he packed a lot into it. His nine symphonies and hundreds of songs are a tour de force in the classical music tradition. His most important works for solo performance are his 11 piano sonatas and the *Wanderer Fantasy*. It's in four movements. It is incredibly unique in that it's played without a break.

Schubert aimed to build, build, and keep building the

sound to the point where the piece drives toward a thunderous ending. I mentioned earlier as the showiest show person of the mid-1800s, Franz Liszt and other composers later adopted this form.

Recommended Listening

Franz Schubert, *Piano Sonata No. 21 in B-flat Major*
Alfred Brendel, Soloist
www.youtube.com/watch?v=TKy0Lyl4g-s

Schubert and Mendelssohn, I must confess, don't first come to mind when I think of the premier solo pianists of their day. It's Frederic Chopin (Poland, 1810-49).

His major big-ticket works are two piano concertos. He wrote no symphonies or operas. He was a solo pianist's pianist. Chopin is given lots of credit for providing the piano with a free, almost spontaneous sound. His 27 **etudes** and 24 **preludes** (1830s)and his n**octurnes, ballades, mazurkas,** and w**altzes** (all dance melodies) are standard teaching and learning pieces for piano students and teachers. His preludes and concert etudes and nocturnes (1827-46) always sound loose and relaxed, with a lot of variety. The feel and spirit of his native homeland, Poland, comes through in his **ballades** (1831-42).

Mazurka is a quick-paced Polish musical form based on stylized folk dances.

Etude is usually a short piece for solo instrument, and the piano is mainly played for the artists' pleasure or as a practice piece.

Recommended Listening

Frederick Chopin, *Mazurka No. 4 in B Minor,* Op. 33
www.youtube.com/watch?v=Z0fFWBWRCWo

* * * * *

Chopin, Mendelssohn, Liszt, Rachmaninoff had good company in another of the solo greats, Robert Schumann (Germany, 1810-56). His four symphonies, a cello concerto, and one grand-scale piano concerto are genuine masterpieces of beauty and power. However, Schumann composed several short character pieces for piano. One of his best-known major piano works, *Carnaval No. 9* (1834-35), conjures up a picture of a masquerade ball.

The pieces paint a vivid picture for the listener of the musical images of well, a carnival, or at least a joyful and amusing experience, with an element of musical puzzle added. They are 20 short pieces in dance rhythm, named for a dance or costumed figure. Schumann liked the program idea so much that it crops up repeatedly in his piano works, making for vivid listening. He and Chopin weren't just playing notes. They were telling a story with and on the solo piano.

🎧 Recommended Listening

Robert Schumann, *Carnaval*, Op. 9
Boris Giltburg, Piano
www.youtube.com/watch?v=LNo2aiKV-a0

From the Concert Seat

Ever wonder why orchestras tune-up? Schumann took a stab at conducting, but he wasn't very successful. On the other hand, Mendelssohn was hailed as one of the truly great conductors of the day during his stint as conductor of one of Europe's greatest orchestras then and now, the Leipzig Gewandhaus Orchestra. Both men had to deal with one aspect of the orchestra that concertgoers are familiar with: the tune-up.

The concertmaster strides to the stage before the conductor and plays a tuning note for the rest of the musicians to match. The tuning instrument is the oboe, in the note of A. The idea is to make sure all the instruments are in sync and playing on key.

Some claim this is done just for show, mostly to please the expectant audience, since the orchestra should already have tuned up before hitting the stage. Others say it's necessary to tune onstage to ensure everyone is hitting the right key. Regardless, tradition is tradition, and it will likely continue, no matter the reason.

Many solo piano works are transcriptions of other composers' songs, symphonies, and operatic paraphrases of songs on popular opera. This was not uncommon. Great composers then and now have always been fascinated with the works of other composers. If the material from another sounds good and plays well, they see no problem with transcribing it and using it in another musical form.

Here's a final note on the soloist. Bach, Mozart, and Beethoven mainly composed smaller works as solo works for themselves. There's Bach's *Goldberg Variations* and *Well-Tempered Clavier*, I mentioned before. He was a master keyboard artist, so it was only natural that he spotlighted his virtuosity on the keyboards. He accomplished this by making the notes sparkle in all keys, with lots of variety, offering a unique sound that has made great listening for three centuries.

Mozart's style is a little different. He lets the musical themes unfold naturally and spontaneously. His notes are measured and often extended to achieve the maximum listening effect. He is also great at conveying feeling and much variety in the piano sound.

He was one of the world's best natural opera composers, if not the world's best. This comes through in many of his piano works which are song-like. Again, a great composer can make the listener see the song-like quality in them rather than simply hearing it.

Recommended Listening

Wolfgang Amadeus Mozart, *Piano Concerto in E* (1785)
Daniel Barenboim, Piano
English Chamber Orchestra
www.youtube.com/watch?v=8hgaxI3JRgg

I've given a thumbnail sketch of the instruments, the composers and their symphonies, concertos, operas, and smaller works, as well as the periods that broadly cover the evolution of classical music. Now I come back to the questions I started with, which have provoked debate, discussion, and anguish in the classical music world. That's why the absence of young persons in the classical music concert halls?

This question strikes at classical music's future.

Conclusion

This debate over why so many younger persons don't like or are not interested in classical music has raged for years. I listed four headlines in the introduction to this book from articles that agonized over why so many young persons don't like, won't listen to, understand, or have no interest in learning about classical music. The articles gave several reasons for the non-appearance of younger persons at classical music concerts and why they don't listen to classical music works. They warned that this spells disaster for the future of classical music.

The National Endowment for the Arts reported that in 2012, only 8.8% of Americans had attended a classical music performance in the previous 12 months, compared to 11.6% a decade earlier. "Older Americans are the only demographic group to show an increase in attendance over a decade ago," the NEA study found.

A Wikipedia-published survey of operagoers found the same greying problem with audiences two years earlier. The flagship Metropolitan Opera the Met) reported that the average age of its audience was 60. Many opera companies attempted to attract a younger audience to halt the more significant trend of greying audiences for classical music since the last decades of the 20th century. Their efforts lowered the average age of the Met's audience to 58 in 2018, the average age at Berlin State Opera was reported as 54, and the Paris Opera reported the same age demographic.

One cynic even claimed that only about one percent of adults like classical music.

The most obvious worry is a financial loss to orchestras from not replenishing the audience stock. However, that's not the only one. Classical music has a long, storied, and honored place in the history and evolution of Western music. It has influenced nearly every musical genre—pop, rock, R&B, jazz, bluegrass, country and western music, and religious music. It has been a training ground for legions of musicians in these areas of music.

Classical music is an intimate part of the cultural tapestry of the West. It is also a major growth industry in interest, performance attendance, and musical sales in many parts of the non-Western world. This alone is reason enough for handwringing about the alleged absence of young persons interested in classical music. So, what to do.?

* * * * *

Start with facing this painful fact. Classical music is a specialized genre of music with its own set of rules, formula, and structure that stretches back hundreds of years. It's in every sense, old, old, old.

You can't cajole, prod, and browbeat a young person into liking something they haven't been regularly exposed to or may be exposed to and don't like. The cajoling won't suddenly cause them to have a Saul on the Road to Damascus epiphany about how great it is to know and like classical music.

Think about it another way. Many people, not just old folk but young people, don't like Pop music. They don't like bluegrass. They don't like country and western. They don't like R&B. In fact, and there are legions of persons of all ages that don't like any music one can think of whether they are exposed to it or not. Classical music is no different or a special exception to the like or don't like rule about music. It's part a matter of personal taste, as much as exposure.

Conclusion

Making concerts shorter or giving away cheap or free tickets isn't going to radically drive up the number of young people rushing to the concert halls. The more realistic goal then is to try and present classical music to the young who show interest as music that can be likable and enjoyable. This means making it music that is understandable. Doing this takes the anguish of trying to make who goes or doesn't like classical music into a numbers game.

From the Concert Seat

Once concert sticks out in mind as a reminder of the profound power of classical music to trumpet the universal spirit of humanity. The occasion was a concert by the Armenian National Philharmonic Orchestra. It was billed as "A Concert of Remembrance" on the one-hundredth anniversary of the estimated one million Armenian victims of the 1915 Turkish initiated holocaust. The concert was moving, emotional, and often tearful. The orchestra with its dynamic playing of Armenian composers Aram Khachaturian's *Spartacus Suite* (1955-57) and Tigran Masurian's *Violin Concerto* captured all the sorrow, pathos, memory, and yet vision of hope a century later of yet another of the world's grotesque genocidal outrages inflicted on an innocent people.

As I listened to the music. I thought, what better way to commemorate the suffering of a people whose spirit remained unbroken than with this music.

It proved again that classical music can and has been both a beacon of monumental hope and a source of magnificent enlightenment in a world that has at times throughout the ages been desperately short of both. It is one more reason that I sing the praise of classical music. I did again that night.

Let's deal with those two goals—exposure and understanding. My interest is not making new converts among the young to classical music. I said, in the beginning, it is to provide a small degree of understanding of some of the parts of classical music—for those interested. If lucky, maybe that alone might add a few more interested parties to the club.

There was a time when schools exposed kids to classical music. There were music classes where instructors played classical pieces, encouraged, and taught students to play instruments, and often arranged field trips for the kids to attend classical concerts. Sadly, those days at most schools are long past. If the schools can't or won't create the musical environment that stirs interest in classical music, then the environment will have to be created elsewhere. The obvious elsewhere is parents, caregivers, or role model adults.

It could be something as simple as playing a classical music piece in the home or car, even if just for a few minutes. Yes, kids that have grown up on rock, rap, *YouTube* texting, and snap chat might squirm and make faces. They may even mutter in protest. But at least having the music on lets them know that the music exists and that the adult of record in the young persons' life thinks it's worthwhile listening.

If there is even a spark of interest, cautiously edge a little further. Tell a little bit about the piece. It's not necessary to be a classical musicologist for this. The announcers, before playing a piece, usually give you the basics. That's the name of the work, the orchestra, and the conductor, and maybe an interesting little factoid about the work or the composer. Repeat all or part of that to the interested young person. The key is repetition. Do that enough times, and at the very least, this gives them some familiarity with the sound of the music.

* * * * *

There are tons of classical music pieces in the public domain. They are played in commercials, ads, movie soundtracks, and TV shows. When you hear a work played in any of them, seize the moment and point out that classical music is not just a bunch of dead European guys way back in the day making music that no one cares about anymore. It's still very much a part of our musical culture and life, whether one hates it or is indifferent to it.

If a young person shows genuine interest, it's time to suggest a trip to a concert. Some orchestras have young-person concerts on Saturdays. They are short, play popular works, and often a speaker makes a few witty remarks about the work, the instruments, and the composer. A good follow-up is to ask them a question or two afterward about what they thought of the event, the instruments, the music, the players, the conductor, or anything. Let them tell you without inserting your opinion.

Young persons today are visual. There's *YouTube*. There's not a work of classical music that's not on YouTube somewhere, either an entire classical work or a part of a work. Compile a shortlist of a few of the abbreviated works on YouTube and encourage them to take a look at it on a cell, iPhone, or desktop.

miniVIRTUOSO has compiled a *YouTube* list of 21 famous classical music works that are likely to have the greatest appeal to young persons. Here's one example. Strauss' *Also Sprach Zarathustra* (1896). The work's opening has been used so many times that it almost needs no introduction. Many young persons would instantly recognize it. It got immortal popularity as the opening of Stanley Kubrick's epic space film *2001: A Space Odyssey*. Since then, it's been a perennial listener crowd-pleaser beyond the classical music arena.

The others listed also have a lot of crossover appeal in

films, commercials, and TV shows. This is another chance to show that classical music is not just long, tedious stuff for old fogies.

 **Recommended Listening**

Richard Strauss, *Also Sprach Zarathustra,* Op. 30
Chicago Symphony Orchestra
www.youtube.com/watch?v=IFPwm0e_K98

* * * * *

The trick is to provide an environment for classical music that makes it fun to listen to, not a chore to listen to. No pressure, no demand, no adult rank pulling allowed. That guarantees to turn classical music into a dreaded enemy. It's just casual, relaxed, and matter-of-fact exposure to the music. This is a step toward making classical music something not scorned, dreaded, and ignored. It can transform into another part of a young person's listening repertoire and rap, hip-hop, reggae, R& B.

My main reason for *A Young Person's Guide to Classical Music* is to provide a simple, easy-to-read survey of classical music and its many parts. I'm not interested in getting loads of young people into the orchestra concert halls. I am interested only in increasing understanding of the music—for those interested.

Notes

Introduction

Vincent Dowd, "Tough Times Ahead for US Orchestras," BBC News, July 25, 2012 www.bbc.com/news/entertainment-arts-18970700

Neybal Maysaud, "It's Time to Let Classical Music Die," Newmusicbox, nd https://nmbx.newmusicusa.org/its-time-to-let-classical-music-die/

Betsy Schwarm, "The Young Persson's Guide to the Orchestra," Britannica, nd www.genius.com/Benjamin-britten-the-young-persons-guide-to-the-orchestra-lyrics

Ellen Fagan, "Young People's Concerts: No Small Part of Leonard Bernstein's Legacy," culturesonar, September 15, 2018 www.culturesonar.com/young-peoples-concerts-no-small-part-of-leonard-bernsteins-legacy/

Leonard Bernstein, "What is a Melody," Leonard Bernstein Lectures, December 21, 1962
www.leonardbernstein.com/lectures/television-scripts/young-peoples-concerts/what-is-melody

The Classical Music Periods

www.azquotes.com/author/21052-George_Frideric_Handel
Merriam-Webster Dictionary, "baroque,"
 www.merriam-webster.com/dictionary/baroque

"Johannes Brahms Quotes," nd
www.azquotes.com/author/1805-Johannes_Brahms

"Handel". Classic FM, nd
www.classicfm.com/composers/handel/guides/handel-facts-composer/beethoven-handel-quote/

Lindsay Kemp, "How Mozart Loved Handel," Gramaphone, January 1, 2015
www.gramophone.co.uk/other/article/how-mozart-loved-handel

"Bach: badass of Counterpoint," A Matter of Music, nd www.listenlearnanddo.wordpress.com/2013/02/11/bach-badass-of-counterpoint/

Wright, Craig, The Essential Listening to Music, (New Haven: Yale University, 2016)
—The Essential Listening to Music, 229

"Johann Strauss in 7 Beautiful Waltzes," Culturetrip, nd www.theculturetrip.com/europe/austria/articles/johann-strauss-in-7-beautiful-waltzes/

"Nineteenth Century Musical Nationalism: Important Milestones Essay," ivypanda, nd
www.ivypanda.com/essays/nineteenth-century-musical-nationalism-important-milestones/

"Beethoven's Classical Inheritance: the Symphony and the Orchestra," Eastman School of Music, nd
www.esm.rochester.edu/beethoven/orchestra-discussions/

"19 Blacks Composers who have shaped the Classical Music World," Classicfm, nd
www.classicfm.com/discover-music/black-musicians-pioneering-in-classical-music/

The Symphony

Shari Mathias, "What is a Symphony," Parker Symphony Orchestra, May 18, 2016, www.parkersymphony.org/what-is-a-symphony

"Elements of Orchestral Music: Instrument Sections, Format and Roles,"study.com, nd www.study.com/academy/lesson/elements-of-orchestral-music-instrument-sections-format-and-roles.html

Victoria Longdon, "Why do Orchestras Need a Conductor," classicfm, March 25, 2021 www.classicfm.com/discover-music/instruments/conductor/what-does-a-conductor-actually-do/music scholar

Serina Sandhu, "Beethoven's Famous Fifth Symphony Opening was nearly abandoned, says Music Scholar," msn, nd
www.msn.com/en-us/music/news/beethoven-s-famous-fifth-symphony-opening-was-nearly-abandoned-says-music-scholar/ar-AATgm0O

"Symphony No, 2 "Little Russian" www.laphil.com/musicdb/pieces/3941/symphony-no-2-little-russian

David Brown, Tchaikovsky: The Early Years, (New York: Norton, 1979) 259-260

"15 Quotes from Leonard Bernstein," kidadl, November 4, 2021

www.kidadl.com/articles/leonard-bernstein-quotes-from-the-composer-of-west-side-story

The Concerto

Stephen Whitehead, "The Patronage that Never Was: J.S. Bach, the Earl of Brandenburg and Six Concertos ," Tristan Arts Blog, May 31, 2011

www.tristanarts.wordpress.com/2011/05/31/the-patronage-that-never-was-j-s-bach-the-earl-of-brandenburg-and-six-concertos-by-stephen-whitehead/

"Concerto," Britannica, nd
www.britannica.com/art/concerto-music

"What is the Essence of a Concerto," lisbdnet, nd
www.lisbdnet.com/what-is-the-essence-of-a-classical-concerto/

Michael Beek, "What is the difference between a concerto and a symphony," classicalmusic, July 21, 2021
www.classical-music.com/features/articles/what-is-the-difference-between-a-concerto-and-a-symphony/

"What makes Rachmaninoff's Piano Concerto #3 so difficult?" quora, nd
www.quora.com/What-makes-Rachmaninoffs-3rd-

Concerto-so-difficult
www.wikipedia.org/wiki/Brandenburg_Concertos

www.wikipedia.org/wiki/Piano_concertos_by_Wolfgang_Amadeus_Mozart

The Opera

"Verdi Quotes," quotikon, nd
www.quoteikon.com/giuseppe-verdi-quotes.html
"The Interesting History of Opera," mentalitch, nd
www.mentalitch.com/the-interesting-history-of-opera/

What are the Different Voice Types?, operaspace, nd
www.operaspace.org/learn/voice-types/

"Houston Grand Opera takes 'The Magic Flute' into the Roaring 1920s," Houston Chronicle, nd
www.newskudo.com/texas/houston/entertainment/7688035-houston-grand-opera-takes-the-magic-flute-into-the-roaring-1920s

Betsy Schwarm, "Der Ring des Nibelungen." Brittanica, nd www.britannica.com/topic/Der-Ring-des-Nibelungen

Julie, "HowDid Verismo opera reflect the ideas of realism," Malaysian Digest, November 14, 2021 www.malaysiandigest.com/how-did-verismo-opera-reflect-the-ideas-of-realism/

"Similarities and differences between musicals and operas and the different eras of music," August 20, MYP Music, 2015 www.mypmusicbryan.wordpress.com/2015/08/20/similarities-and-differences-between-musicals-and-operas-and-the-different-eras-of-music/

"What are the greatest Opera Overtures," classicalmusiconly, nd www.classicalmusiconly.com/recommendation/what-are-the-greatest-opera-overtures-84aab76d

"69 Top Richard Wagner Quotes, " thefamouspeople, nd https://quotes.thefamouspeople.com/richard-wagner-392.php

The Smaller Works

"Contemplating Beethoven's String Quartet Op. 131 & Its Inexhaustible Originality," Strings, April 2. 2019 www.stringsmagazine.com/contemplating-beethovens-op-131-its-inexhaustible-originality/

"Sonata Form," Milne Library nd
https://milnepublishing.geneseo.edu/fundamentals-function-form/chapter/38-sonata-form/
"Sonata," Wikipedia, nd
www.wikipedia.org/wiki/Sonata

"Sonata Form," Music Academy Theory, nd
www.musictheoryacademy.com/understanding-music/sonata-form/

"What is a... Trio, " classicalmusic, June 10, 2016
www.classical-music.com/features/articles/what-trio/

"What is a String Quartet?" classicalmusic, June 9, 2016
www.classical-music.com/features/articles/what-string-quartet/

The Instruments

"26 Plus Best Quotes from Bach," kidadl, nd
www.kidadl.com/articles/best-johann-sebastian-bach-quotes-from-the-famous-german-composer

Michael Beek, "The violin: when it was invented, who made them and how it has changed throughout history, classical-music, March 30, 2021

"The Classical Period," Britannica, nd
www.britannica.com/art/instrumentation-music/

The-Classical-period
www.classical-music.com/features/articles/violin-facts-and-invention

"Wind instruments," Musicworld, nd
www.music-world.org/woodwinds

"Brass Instruments,"Musicworld, nd
www.music-world.org/wind-instruments-brass

"What is a Percussion instrument?" classicfm, nd
www.classicfm.com/discover-music/instruments/percussion/

"Keyboard Instruments," Musicworld, nd
www.music-world.org/keyboards-piano

"Symphony Fantastique,"J1
 Wikipedia, nd
www.wikipedia.org/wiki/Symphonie_fantastique

"Hector Berlioz's Treatise on instrumentation and orchestration,"viola-in-music.com, nd
www.viola-in-music.com/treatise-on-instrumentation.html

The Soloist

"Piano Concerto No. 3 (Rachmaninoff), Wikipedia, nd
www.wikipedia.org/wiki/Piano_Concerto_No._3_(Rachmaninoff)

Solo, Wikipedia, nd
www.wikipedia.org/wiki/Solo_(music)

"Felix Mendelssohn," Biography, nd
www.biography.com/musician/felix-mendelssohn

Justin Wildridge, "5 Famous Piano Pieces by WA Mozart," cmuse, February 12, 2019
www.cmuse.org/mozart-famous-piano-pieces/

"Franz Schubert," Biography, nd
www.biography.com/artist/franz-schubert

"Best Schumann Works: 10 Essential Pieces By The Great Composer,"udiscovermusic, June 7, 2021
www.udiscovermusic.com/classical-features/best-schumann-works-10-essential-pieces/

Maddy Shaw Roberts, "Why do Orchestra Tune to an "A"?, classicfm, September 13, 2018
www.classicfm.com/discover-music/instruments/oboe/features/orchestras-tune-to-oboe/

"Carnaval," ms, nd
www.morissenegor.com/musical-conversations/schumann-carnaval-1835/

Conclusion

Phyllis Feng, "Is Classical Music on the Decline?" Affinity, January 12, 2019
www.culture.affinitymagazine.us/is-classical-music-on-the-decline/

Charlie Albright, "Classical' music is dying…and that's the best thing for classical music, " CNN, May 29, 2016
www.cnn.com/2016/05/29/opinions/classical-music-dying-and-being-reborn-opinion-albright/index.html

Also sprach Zarathustra, Wikipedia, nd
www.wikipedia.org/wiki/Also_sprach_Zarathustra

James Milner, "21 Best Pieces of Classical Music for Kids," miniVirtuouso, March 26, 2019
www.minivirtuoso.com/21-best-pieces-of-classical-music-for-kids/

Index

Adagio defined, 38
A History of Western Music, 13
Allegro defined, 37
Also Sprach Zarathustra, 124
Alto Soprano defined, 70

Bach, Johann Sebastian, 4, 10-11, 13, 16, 48-49, 58-59, 96, 115
    Brandenburg Concertos, six, 58-60, 88
    Letter to Margrave, 48
Baritone defined, 70
Baroque Period, 10
Basso Continuo defined, 11
Bass defined, 70
Beethoven, Ludwig Von, 3, 13, 44, 82
    Master pianist, 54, 87
    Moonlight Sonata, 83-84
    Piano Concerto No. 5 "Emperor," 57
    String Quartet in C-sharp Minor, 37
    Symphony No. 3 "Eroica," 26

Symphony No. 6 "Pastoral," 21
Symphony No. 7, 33
Symphony No. 9 "Choral," 39
Bel canto, 69
Berlioz, Hector, 44, 104-105
Symphonie Fantastique, 106-107
Bernstein, Leonard, 4, 5, 6, 7, 9, 76
Candide, 77
Young Peoples Concerts, 7, 8
Bizet, George, 25, 76
Carmen, 76
Brahms, Johannes, 13, 44
Brass Instruments, 101-103
French Horn
Trombone
Tuba
Bridgetower, George, 88-89
Britten, Benjamin, 3, 8
Young Person's Guide to the Orchestra, 8
Bryant, Kobe, 84
Plays Beethoven's *Moonlight Sonata,* 83

Cadenza defined, 54
Cantata defined, 14
Cello, 99
Copland, Aaron, 29-30
Chopin, Frederick, 114
Chorus defined, 64

Classical Period, 17
Classical Music Specialized, 119-121
Classical Music and Young Persons, 121-123
Coloratura defined, 70
Concerto defined, 51
Concerto, 49-62
Conductor-less Orchestras, 37
Counterpoint defined, 16
Crescendo defined, 107

Debussy, Claude, 22
    La Mer, 22
    Prelude to the Afternoon of a Faun, 22
Development defined, 39
Diva defined, 69
Divo defined, 69
Double bass defined, 99
Dvorak, Antonin, 27-29
    Symphony No. 9 "From the New World"

Elgar, Edward, 28
Etudes defined, 114
Exposition defined, 40

Fantasia defined, 18
Frequencies defined, 15, 97
Fugue defined, 16, 83
Full Anthem defined, 15

Gershwin, George, 29-30, 76
 Porgy and Bess, 77
Gounod, Charles, 25
Grand Opera defined, 67

Handel, George Frederick, 10, 13
 Messiah, 10
Haydn, Franz Joseph, 3, 25, 41, 92, 98
 String Quartet in D Minor, 94
High Baroque, 10

Impressionist Painters and Classical Music, 20-21
 Cezanne
 Monet
 Picasso
Impressionist Composers, 22-23
 Albeniz, Jacque
 Debussy, Claude
 Delius, Frederick
 de Falla, Manuel
 Ravel, Maurice
 Respighi, Ottorino
Introduction defined, 40

Key defined, 40
Keyboards, 103-105
 Piano

Grand Piano
Upright Piano
Kubrick, Stanley, 124
    2001: A Space Odyssey (film), *Also Sprach Zarathustra*

Leitmotif defined, 73
Libretto defined, 73
Liszt, Franz, 56, 111

Madrigal defined, 11
Mahler, Gustav, 32, 34, 45, 98
    Symphony No. 2 "The Resurrection," 39
Major keys defined, 33
Masque defined, 15
Mass defined, 14
Mazurka defined, 110
Melody defined, 17
Mendelssohn, Felix, 42, 109, 110, 111-112
    A *Midsummer Night's Dream,* 109
Messiah, 15
Minor keys defined, 33
Minuet defined, 38
Modernism, 31
Movements defined, 38-39
Monteverdi, Claudio, 72
Mozart, Wolfgang Amadeus, 3, 4, 54, 60, 115
    Don Giovanni, 73
    Magic Flute, 73

Master pianist, 54
Musical Genres, 8, 118, 125
- Bluegrass
- Country and Western
- Hip Hop
- Jazz
- Pop
- R&B
- Rap
- Reggae

National Endowment for the Arts Study, 118
Nocturne defined, 18
Numbers defined, 85

Opera, 63-81
Opus defined, 64
Overture defined, 64
Opera Comique, 67
Opera Bouffe, 67

Percussion Instruments, 102-103
- Bass drum
- Cymbal
- Gong
- Snare drum
- Timpani
- Triangle

Piano, 103
Pitches defined, 103
Pizzicato defined, 100
Prelude defined, 18
Pretty Woman (film) and Opera Theme, 76
Price, Florence, 30
Puccini, Giacomo, 76-77
    La Boheme
    Madama Butterfly
    Tosca

Quartet defined, 91-94

Recapitulation defined, 40
Recitative, 72
Rondo, 38
Rush, Geoffrey, *Shine*, 55
Rachmaninoff, Sergei
    Piano Concerto No. 3, 55
Russian composers, 25-26, 29, 53, 111
    Prokofiev, Sergei
    Rachmaninoff, Sergei
    Rimsky-Korsakov, Nicholai
    Shostakovich, Dmitri
Saint-Saens, Camille, 25
    Symphony No. 3 "The Organ," 25
Schubert, Franz, 44, 112-113
Schumann, Robert, 44

Score defined, 51
Seasons defined, 72
Sibelius, Jean, 28, 29
Singspiel defined, 68
Solo, 110
Soloist, 109-118
Sonata defined, 36
Still, William Grant, 30
Strauss, Johann, 23-24
 Waltzes, 23
Strauss, Richard, 23, 44
Stravinsky, Igor, 26-27
 Rite of Spring, 26
String Instruments, 97-100
 Cello
 Double bass
 Viola
 Violin
Symphony, 32-48
Symphony Orchestra, 34-35
Symphony Movements, 37-39

Tchaikovsky, Peter Ilyich, 24, 45-47
 Symphony No. 2 "Little Russian," 46-47
Telemann, Georg Philipp, 12
Tenor defined, 70
Tone Poem, 20, 44
Trio defined, 89-91

Verdi, Giuseppe, 63, 75-76, 80
    Aida
    Falstaff
    Macbeth
    Otello
Verismo defined, 75
Viola, 99
Violin, 97
Vivaldi, Antonio, 10, 16
von Weber, Carl Maria, 70, 71, 77

Wagner, Richard, 68, 73-75, 78, 79, 80-81
    Flying Dutchman
    Lohengrin
    Ring Cycle
    Tannhauser
Woodwinds, 100-101
    Bassoon
    Flute
    Oboe
    Piccolo

YouTube and Classical Music, 124

Bibliography

Abbate, Carolyn. *A History of Opera*. (New York: W. W. Norton & Company, 2012).

Alexander, Morin, ed. *Classical Music: Third Ear: The Essential Listening Companion*. (Milwaukee: Backbeat Books, 2002).

Berger, William. *NPR The Curious Listener's Guide to Opera*. (New York: Perigee Trade, 2002).

Bernstein, Leonard. *The Leonard Bernstein Letters* (New Haven: Yale University Press, 2014)

Bookspan, Martin. *101 Masterpieces of Music & Their Composers*. (New York: Dolphin Books,1964)

Burton, Humphrey, *Leonard Bernstein* Paperback (New York: Humphrey Burton, 2001)

Copland, Aaron. *What to Listen for in Music*, Reissue. (New York: Signet, 2011).

Dubai, David. *The Essential Canon of Classical Music*, 1st Edition. (New York: North Point Press; 2003)

Goulding G., Phil. *Classical Music: The 50 Greatest Composers and Their 1,000 Greatest Works.* (New York: Ballantine Books, 2011).

Greenberg, Robert. *How to Listen to Great Music: A Guide to Its History, Culture, and Heart.* (New York: Penguin Books, 2011)

Beethoven and Me Jacobson, Julius H. II. *The Classical Music Experience.* (Sourcebooks, Naperville, Illinois, 2002)

Libbey, Ted. *The NPR Guide to Building a Classical CD Collection: The 350 Essential Works,* 2nd Edition. (New York: Workman Publishing Company, 1999)

Mordden, Ethan. *A Guide to Orchestral Music: The Handbook for Non-Musicians,* 1st Edition. (New York: Oxford University Press, 1986)

Pogue, David and Speck, Scott. *Classical Music for Dummies.* (New York: Wiley Publishing, 1997

Rosen, Charles. *Sonata Forms,* Revised Edition. (New York: W. W. Norton & Company, 1988).

Rosen, Charles. *The Classical Style: Haydn, Mozart, Beethoven.* (New York: W. W. Norton & Co., 1998)

Ross, Alex. *The Rest Is Noise: Listening to the Twentieth Century.* (New York: Farrar, Straus and Giroux, 2007).

Rye, Matthew, ed. *1001 Classical Recordings You Must Hear Before You Die.* (New York: Universe Publishing, 2008).

Staines, Joe. *The Rough Guide to Classical Music,* Rev. Edition. (U. K.: Rough Guides, 5 Exp, 2010).

Steinberg, Michael. *The Symphony: A Listener's Guide,* Reprint Edition. (New York: Oxford University Press, 1998)

Swafford, Jan. *The Vintage Guide to Classical Music.* (New York: Vintage Books, 1992)

Veinus, Abraham. *The Concerto: From Its Origins to the Modern Era.* (New York: Dover Publications, 2012).

Talking the Classical Music's Jargon

Aria. This is an impassioned song in which soprano, tenor, or bass can be heard within an opera production. Some very creative individuals figured out that aria can also be for a solo instrument too. Bach spruced up parts of his piano sites with an aria.

Cadenza. This is how a concert virtuoso performer really shows off his or her stuff. The soloist can deviate from the score. The chords and notes can be written for them, or they may write their own and take off on any flight of musical fancy that suits them. That flight can last for just a few seconds or several minutes. Meanwhile, the orchestra and conductor wait patiently for them to finish, then jump back in.

Canon. This is a piece of music in which two or more voices (instrumental parts) sing or play the same music, starting at different times. A lot of filmgoers got their first introduction to the canon in the 1980 movie, *Ordinary People,* which Robert Redford earned an Academy Award for directing. The music was the epitome of a gentle, soft, easygoing work. It was *The Canon and Gigue for 3 Violins and Basso Continuo* by German Baroque composer Johann Pachelbel (1653-1706).

Cantata. This is a short religious work for soloists and chorus.

Chorale. This is a Protestant hymn usually sung at church services.

Coda. This is a musical passage(s) that comes after the end of the piece. In the hands of Beethoven, Haydn and Mozart it can take on the force and power of the other parts of the work.

Concerto Grosso. This is Italian for "big concert," though the piece is not always for a big ensemble. There are small ensemble concerto grossi (the plural), with the soloists tossing the music to the orchestra.

Continuous Bass (Basso Continuo). This keeps the bass line going with a keyboard instrument and another bass instrument such as cello, violone (an old form of double-bass), or bassoon.

Counterpoint. This is absolutely crucial to music, so the definition bears repeating. If you play one melody simultaneously with another, they are playing counter to each other. This is contrapuntal or, more commonly, counterpoint. Think of two dueling singers going at each other at the same time. All composers since then have genuflected to Bach for this. He is the absolute king of the hill of counterpoint.

Development. This section develops the theme(s).

Dissonance. We'll run into this a lot. It literally means a harsh, disagreeable combination of sounds; discord. Music dissonance expresses the jumble of human emotions in sound, a sound that can grate on the nerves of some.

Duet. This is two singers going back and forth.

Exposition. This section of the symphony introduces the symphony's theme or themes or what's sometimes called the composer's idea(s).

Fugue. It's literally a "chase" like to chase after each other. So certain parts or voices interchange at various points after each comes in.

Key. This is t main note of a piece on a scale of pitches. If you see a symphony in the key of D, the main note is the D note.

Libretto. This is the text of the opera.

Madrigal. This is a secular vocal number with no instruments, for anywhere from two to eight singers.

Major and Minor Keys. This is the note scale that starts a composition: in "C Minor" or A Major" and so on. Another way of thinking of it is to remember that the major keys tend to make a happy sound, while the minor keys are more morose.

Melody. This is music that moves in a straight line, one note after another.

Movement. This is a self-contained part of a musical composition or musical form. You'll see and hear a symphony referred to as "first movement," "second movement," and so on.

Motet. This is a choral piece of music for a church service that's sung without any instruments.

Op. (Opus) This is the title and number of a composition.

Oratorio. This is a long, sometimes, very long, religious work for soloists and chorus.

Partita. This is a piece of a single instrument or multiple instruments.

Prelude. This is a short piece of music, actually introductory.

Recapitulation. This section reintroduces the theme(s).

Recitative. This is like talking without music. Rap is recitative, for example, but for our purposes, it's a predominant form in opera and religious verses, one in which the singer talks between numbers.

Rondo. This is a musical theme that returns over and over and contrasts with another theme.

Scherzo. This is a quick-paced, frolicking sound, sometimes called musically humorous.

Sinfonia. This is the Italian word for the symphony.

Toccata. This is a nimble, fast piece of music that's great for displaying an artist's virtuosity.

Variations and **Suite.** The first is altering or varying the musical material. In other words, to change the mood. The other is a musical piece that pairs several dance tunes.

About the Author

Earl Ofari Hutchinson is the host of the weekly Pacifica Radio show *Classical Composers & Compositions*. He has an M.A. in Humanities from California State University, Dominguez Hills that included the Humanities course series on the advanced study of music, focusing on concepts of meaning and form in music. He is a member Emeritus of the American Musicological Society. He has for a decade programed, featured, and promoted classical music on the KPFK-Pacifica Radio Network.

From 1995 to 2015, he attended nearly 500 concerts by nearly every nationally and internationally known major orchestra, and that featured many of the top virtuoso performers, and attended many major festivals including the Aspen, Bach Carmel, and the Ojai Festival. He has interviewed many of the leading classical conductors, composers, and performers.

He has written about classical musical developments in his columns. He moderated the prestigious panel of classical artists and musicologists on the works of Dimitri Shostakovich. He has attended and participated in numerous concert lectures and preconcert lectures. He completed the Comprehensive Music Study Series based on The History of Western Music at West Los Angeles College and studied music theory and history at the Pasadena Conservatory of Music. He has earned certificates in advanced classical music appreciation from Yale University and Udemy Online.

www.ingramcontent.com/pod-product-compliance
Lightning Source LLC
Chambersburg PA
CBHW030438010526
44118CB00011B/694